T0155637

Advanced Applied Deep Learning

Convolutional Neural Networks and Object Detection

Umberto Michelucci

Apress®

Advanced Applied Deep Learning: Convolutional Neural Networks and Object Detection

Umberto Michelucci
TOELT LLC, Dübendorf, Switzerland

ISBN-13 (pbk): 978-1-4842-4975-8   ISBN-13 (electronic): 978-1-4842-4976-5
https://doi.org/10.1007/978-1-4842-4976-5

Managing Director, Apress Media LLC: Welmoed Spahr
Acquisitions Editor: Celestin Suresh John
Development Editor: Matthew Moodie
Coordinating Editor: Aditee Mirashi

Cover designed by eStudioCalamar

Cover image designed by Freepik (www.freepik.com)

Distributed to the book trade worldwide by Springer Science+Business Media New York, 233 Spring Street, 6th Floor, New York, NY 10013. Phone 1-800-SPRINGER, fax (201) 348-4505, e-mail orders-ny@springer-sbm.com, or visit www.springeronline.com. Apress Media, LLC is a California LLC and the sole member (owner) is Springer Science + Business Media Finance Inc (SSBM Finance Inc). SSBM Finance Inc is a **Delaware** corporation.

For information on translations, please e-mail rights@apress.com, or visit http://www.apress.com/rights-permissions.

Apress titles may be purchased in bulk for academic, corporate, or promotional use. eBook versions and licenses are also available for most titles. For more information, reference our Print and eBook Bulk Sales web page at http://www.apress.com/bulk-sales.

Any source code or other supplementary material referenced by the author in this book is available to readers on GitHub via the book's product page, located at www.apress.com/978-1-4842-4975-8. For more detailed information, please visit http://www.apress.com/source-code.

Printed on acid-free paper

This book is dedicated to my wife Francesca and daughter Caterina, who always show me how important it is to have dreams and to follow them.

Table of Contents

About the Author

 **Umberto Michelucci** studied physics and mathematics. He is an expert in numerical simulation, statistics, data science, and machine learning. Over the years, he has continuously expanded his expertise in post-graduate courses and research projects. In addition to several years of research experience at George Washington University (USA) and the University of Augsburg (DE), he has 15 years of practical experience in data warehouse, data science, and machine learning. He is currently responsible for Deep Learning, New Technologies, and Research Cooperation at Helsana Versicherung AG. In 2014, he completed a postgraduate certificate in professional studies in education in England to broaden his knowledge of teaching and pedagogy. He is the author of *Applied Deep Learning: A Case-Based Approach to Understanding Deep Neural Networks,* published by Springer in 2018. He regularly publishes his research results in leading journals and gives lectures at international conferences. He is also a founder of TOELT llc, a company focusing on research in AI in science.

About the Technical Reviewer

 **Jojo Moolayil** is an artificial intelligence professional. He has authored three books on machine learning, deep learning, and IoT. He is currently working with Amazon Web Services as a Research Scientist – A.I. in their Vancouver, BC office.

He was born and raised in Pune, India and graduated from the University of Pune with a major in Information Technology Engineering. His passion for problem-solving and data-driven decision led him to start a career with Mu Sigma Inc., the world's largest pure-play analytics provider. He was responsible for developing machine learning and decision science solutions to large complex problems for Healthcare and Telecom giants. He later worked with Flutura (an IoT analytics startup) and General Electric, with a focus on Industrial A.I in Bangalore, India.

In his current role with AWS, he works on researching and developing large-scale A.I. solutions for combating fraud and enriching the customer payment experience in the cloud. He is also actively involved as a tech reviewer and AI consultant with leading publishers and has reviewed over a dozen books on machine learning, deep learning, and business analytics.

You can reach out to Jojo at

- https://www.jojomoolayil.com/
- https://www.linkedin.com/in/jojo62000
- https://twitter.com/jojo62000

Acknowledgments

Writing this second book on more advanced topics has been a challenge. Finding the right level—finding the right parts to discuss and the right ones to leave out—caused me a few sleepless nights. This would not have been possible without several people who gave me feedback and discussed the chapters with me. I need to thank my editors, from Aditee to Matt, and especially my technical editor Jojo, who read and tried all the code. What patience. The team at Apress has been great. Thanks go to Celestin John, the acquisitions editor, who believed in me. Thanks to everyone for everything; you are great.

Of course, a big thank you goes to my family, who put up with me spending time at the computer writing, testing code, writing more, testing more, and so on and so forth. Thanks to my wife Francesca for her endless patience. I don't know how she put up with me. I really don't. To my daughter Caterina goes a special thank you. She shows me everyday how great it is to love something and do it just for fun, and how important it is not too take yourself too seriously.

A special thanks to all the readers who invested part of their lives reading what I wrote. I am really flattered that you are doing that. I would love to hear from you, so get in touch. You can get in touch with me at umberto.michelucci@toelt.ai, or you use the GitHub repository to get in touch with me by opening an issue. Really, do that. I look forward to hearing from you.

Introduction

This is the second book I have written, and it covers advanced topics in deep learning. It will require some knowledge to be understood. It's not for beginners. If you are one, I suggest you check out my first book published by Apress (*Applied Deep Learning: A Case-Based Approach*, ISBN 978-1-4842-3790-8). To understand this book, you should have some intermediate to advanced experience in Python and some intermediate to advanced deep learning experience (and experience with neural networks in general). This book assumes you know things like regularization, hyperparameter tuning, mini-batch gradient descent, which optimizers are more efficient (does the name Adam tell you something?), and so on. I also use heavily Keras (from TensorFlow), so I suggest you get some experience with that too. It will help you work through the examples of the book.

I tried to tackle advanced topics, like transfer learning or multi-loss function networks, with a practical approach. That means I explain the concepts and then show you how to implement those things in Keras. I invested quite some time in preparing code for you and it's available on the GitHub repository for the book, so get the code and use it while you're reading the book. The code for the advanced topics we deal with, is too long to discuss completely, so I only dissect the most important parts. In GitHub, you have all of it.

This book touches on several research fields, but was not written for very experienced researchers. It has been written for practitioners who want to start doing research; therefore, its goal is to bridge the gap between the beginner and the researcher. Very advanced topics, like in object detection, are not explained in much technical detail, since otherwise the book would turn into a collection of research papers.

Keep in mind that many of the things I describe in the book, like the YOLO object detection algorithm, are only a few years old. For advanced topics, the only way to understand an algorithm is to read the original paper. You should get used to doing that without any book. Here, I try to give you the tools and explain the language that you need to read the research papers. From there, you are on your own.

If you want to proceed further in your deep learning adventure, you should get used to reading research papers. They are not easy to read and will require time. But this book should give you many tools and tips for a head start. Reading this book and understanding *all of it* will put you at the start of your research career. From there on, start reading research papers. Try to repeat what they did if possible (mostly is not, given the infrastructure needed for deep learning, but you can always try). Understanding algorithms and research papers will give you enough knowledge to evaluate libraries and see what others have done, if you are searching for a way to use a specific algorithm in your projects.

I hope you enjoy the book, that you learn something from it, and that it helps you, but more important than anything—I hope you have fun!

—Umberto Michelucci, Zürich, 3rd of July 2019

CHAPTER 1

Introduction and Development Environment Setup

This book assumes that you have some basic know-how in machine learning, neural networks, and TensorFlow.[1] It follows my first book, *Applied Deep Learning: A Case-Based Approach* (ISBN 978-1-4842-3790-8), published by Apress in 2018, and assumes you know and understand what is explained in there. The first volume's goal is to explain the basic concepts of neural networks and to give you a sound basis in deep learning, and this book's goal is to explain more advanced topics, like convolutional and recurrent neural networks. To be able to profit from this book, you should have at least a basic knowledge of the following topics:

- How a single neuron and its components work (activation functions, inputs, weights, and bias)

- How to develop a simple neural network with several layers in Python with TensorFlow or Keras

---

[1]TensorFlow, the TensorFlow logo, and any related marks are trademarks of Google Inc.

© Umberto Michelucci 2019
U. Michelucci, *Advanced Applied Deep Learning*,
https://doi.org/10.1007/978-1-4842-4976-5_1

- What an optimizer is and how it works (at least you should know how gradient descent works)

- Which advanced optimizers are available and how they work (at least RMSProp, Momentum, and Adam)

- What regularization is and what the most common methods are (ℓ_1, ℓ_2, and dropout)

- What hyperparameters are

- How to train a network and which hyper-parameters play an essential role (for example, the learning rate or the number of epochs)

- What hyperparameter tuning is and how to do it

In the next chapters, we switch freely between low-level TensorFlow APIs and Keras (introduced in the next chapter) where needed, to be able to concentrate on the more advanced concepts and not on implementation details. We will not discuss why a specific optimizer works better or how neurons work. If any of that is unclear, you should keep my first book close and use it as a reference.

Additionally, not all the Python code in the book is discussed as extensively as in my first book. You should already understand Python code well. However, all the new concepts are explained. If you have a sound basis, you will understand very well what is going on (and why). This book is not for beginners of deep learning. If you are one, I suggest buying my first book and studying it before starting this one.

I hope that the book will be enjoyable and that you will learn a lot from it. But most of all, I hope it will be fun.

GitHub Repository and Companion Website

The Jupyter Notebooks related to the code I discuss in this book are found on GitHub.[2] To find the link to them, go to the Apress web page for this book. Near the cover of the book, a button with the text "Download Code" can be found. It points to the GitHub repository. The notebooks contain specific topics discussed in the book, including exercises of additional material that did not fit in the book. It is even possible to leave feedback directly on GitHub using "Issues" (see `https://goo.gl/294qg4` to learn how). It would be great to hear from you. The GitHub repository acts as a companion to the book, meaning it contains more code than is printed in the book. If you are a teacher, I hope you can use these notebooks for your students. The notebooks are the same ones I use in my university courses, and much work has gone into making them useful for teaching.

The best way to learn is to try. Don't merely read the book: try, play with the code, change it, and apply it to concrete problems.

A companion website is also available, where news about the book and additional useful material is found. Its URL is `www.applieddeeplearningbook.com`.

Mathematical Level Required

There are a few sections that are more mathematically advanced. You should understand most of these concepts without the mathematical details. However, it is essential to know what a matrix is, how to multiply matrices, what a transpose is, and so on. You basically need a sound grasp of linear algebra. If that is not the case, I suggest reviewing a linear algebra book before reading this book. A basic understanding of calculus is also

---

[2]In case you don't know what GitHub is, you can learn the basics with this guide at `https://guides.github.com/activities/hello-world/`

beneficial. It is important not to skip the mathematical parts. They can help you understand why we do things in specific ways. You should also not be scared by more complex mathematical notations. The goal of this book is not to give you a mathematical foundation; I assume you have that already. Deep learning and neural networks (in general, machine learning) are complex and whoever tries to convince you otherwise is lying or doesn't understand them.

We will not spend time justifying or deriving algorithms or equations. Additionally, we will not discuss the applicability of specific equations. For example, we will not discuss the problem of differentiability of functions when we calculate derivatives. Just assume we can apply the formulas you find here. Many years of practical implementations have shown the deep learning community that those methods and equations work as expected. These kinds of advanced discussions would require a separate book.

Python Development Environment

In this book, we work exclusively with TensorFlow and Keras from Google, and we develop our code exclusively with Jupyter Notebooks, so it is crucial to know how to deal with them. There are three main possibilities when working with the code in the book, and in general when working with Python and TensorFlow:

- Use Google Colab, a cloud-based Python development environment.

- Install a Python development environment locally on a laptop or desktop.

- Use a Docker image provided by Google, with TensorFlow installed.

Let's look at the different options in order to decide which one is the best for you.

Google Colab

As mentioned, Google Colab is a cloud-based environment. That means nothing has to be installed locally. A Google account and a web browser (preferably Google Chrome) are the only things you need. The URL of the service is `https://colab.research.google.com/`.

Just log in with a Google account or create one if you don't have one.

You will then get a window where you can open existing notebooks, if you have some already in the cloud, or create new ones. The window looks like Figure 1-1.

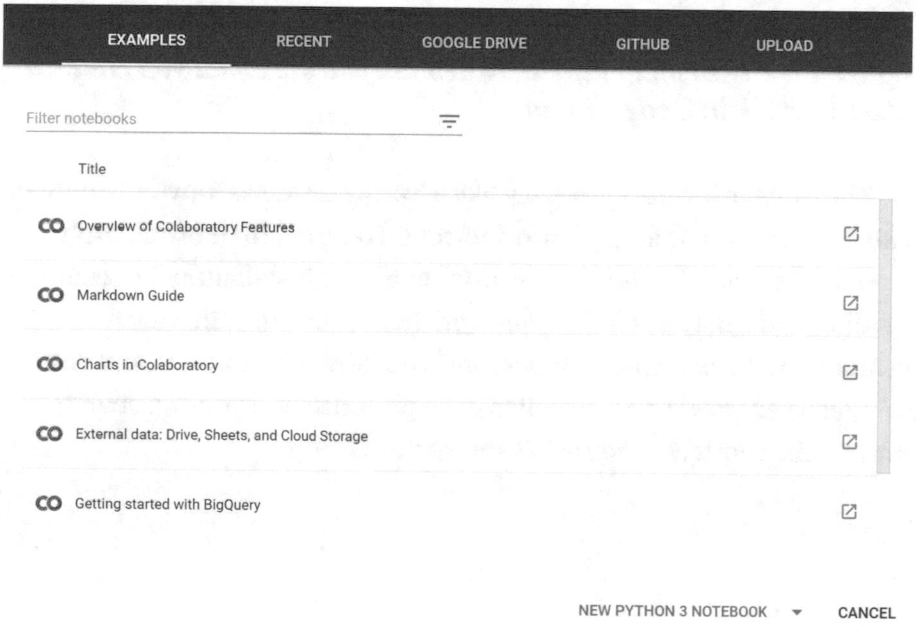

Figure 1-1. *The first screen you see when you log in to Google Colab. In this screenshot, the Recent tab is open. Sometimes the Recent tab is opened the first time you log in.*

In the lower right, you can see the NEW PYTHON 3 NOTEBOOK link (typically in blue). If you click on the small downward triangle, you have the option of creating a Python 2 notebook. In this book, we use Python 3 exclusively. If you click the link, you get an empty Jupyter Notebook, like the one shown in Figure 1-2.

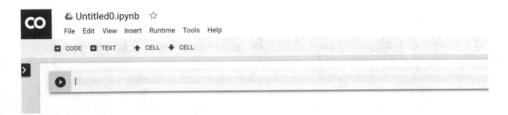

Figure 1-2. *The empty Jupyter Notebook you see when you create a new notebook in Google Colab*

The notebook works precisely like a locally installed Jupyter Notebook, with the exception that keyboard shortcuts (referred to here as simply shortcuts) are not the same as the ones in a local installation. For example, pressing X to delete a cell does not work here (but works in a local installation). In case you are stuck, and you don't find the shortcut you want, you can press Ctrl+Shift+P to get a popup where you can search through the shortcuts. Figure 1-3 shows this popup.

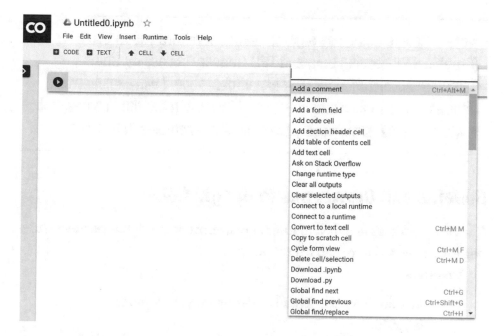

Figure 1-3. *The popup to search keyboard shortcuts when pressing Ctrl+Shift+P. Note that you can type a command name to search for it. You don't need to scroll through them.*

For example, typing DELETE in the popup tells you that, to delete a cell, you need to type Ctrl+M and then D. An exceptional place to start learning what is possible in Google Colab is from this Google notebook:

`https://Colab.research.Google.com/notebooks/basic_features_ overview.ipynb` (`https://goo.gl/h9Co1f`).

Note   Google Colab has a great feature: it allows you to use GPU (Graphical Processing Unit) and TPU (Tensor Processing Unit)[3] hardware acceleration for your experimentation. I will explain what difference this makes and how to use this when the time comes, but it will not be necessary to try the code and examples in this book.

Benefits and Drawbacks to Google Colab

Google Colab is a great development environment, but it has positive and negative aspects. Here is an overview.

Positives:

- You don't have to install anything on your laptop/desktop.

- You can use GPU and TPU acceleration without buying expensive hardware.

- It has excellent sharing possibilities.

- Multiple people can collaboratively edit the same notebook at the same time. Like Google Docs, you can set collaborators both within the document (top right, left of the comments button) and within a cell (right of the cell).[4]

---

[3]In deep learning, most of the calculations are done between tensors (multi-dimensional arrays). GPUs and TPUs are chips that are highly optimized to perform such calculations (like matrix multiplications) between very big tensors (up to a million of elements). When developing networks, it is possible to let GPUs and TPUs perform such expensive calculation in Google Colab, speeding up the training of networks.

[4]Google Colab documentation is found at https://goo.gl/bKNWy8

Negatives:

- You need to be online to use and work with it. If you want to study this book on a train while commuting, you may not be able to do so.

- If you have sensitive data and you are not allowed to upload it to a cloud service, you cannot work with it.

- This system is designed for research and experimentation, so you should not use it as a substitute productive environment.

Anaconda

The second way of using and testing the code in this book is to have a local installation of Python and TensorFlow on your laptop or desktop. The easiest way to do that is using Anaconda. Here I describe in quite some detail how to do that.

To set it up, first download and install Anaconda for your system (I used Anaconda on Windows 10, but the code is not dependent on it, so feel free to use a Mac or Linux version if you prefer). You can get the Anaconda from https://anaconda.org/.

On the right side of the web page (see Figure 1-4), you'll find a Download Anaconda link.

Figure 1-4. *On the top-right side of the Anaconda website, you'll find a link to download the software*

Just follow the instructions to install it. When you start it after the installation, you should see the screen shown in Figure 1-5.

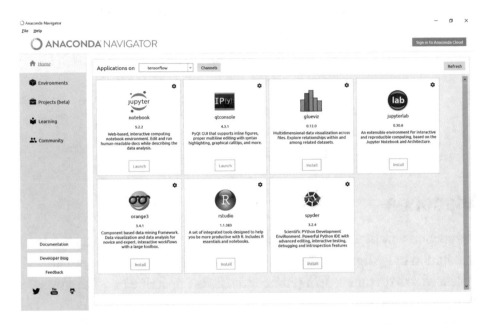

Figure 1-5. *The screen you see when you start Anaconda*

Python packages (like numpy) are updated regularly and very often. A new version of a package may make your code stop working. Functions are deprecated and removed and new ones are added. To solve this problem, in Anaconda you can create what is called an environment. That is a container that contains a specific Python version and specific versions of the packages you decide to install. This way, you can have a container for Python 2.7 and numpy 1.10 and another with Python 3.6 and numpy 1.13, for example. You may have to work with code that exists already, and that is based on Python 2.7, and therefore you need a container with the right Python version. However, at the same time, it may be that for your projects you need Python 3.6. With containers, you can do all this at the same time. Sometimes different packages conflict, so you must be careful, and you should avoid installing all the packages you find interesting in your environment, primarily if you use it for developing under a deadline. There's nothing worse than discovering that your code is not working anymore, and you don't know why.

Note   When you define an environment, try to install only the packages you need and pay attention when you update them to make sure that the upgrade does not break your code (remember that functions are deprecated, removed, added, or changed very often). Check the updates documentation before upgrading and do it only if you need the updated features.

In the first book of the series (`https://goo.gl/ytiQ1k`), I explained how to create an environment with the graphical interface, so you can check that to learn how, or you can read the following page on the Anaconda documentation to understand how to work with environments in detail:

`https://conda.io/docs/user-guide/tasks/manage-environments.html`

In the next section, we will create an environment and install TensorFlow in one shot, with one command only.

Installing TensorFlow the Anaconda Way

Installing TensorFlow is not complicated and has gotten a lot easier in the last year since my last book. To start (we describe the procedure for Windows here), go into the Start menu in Windows and type Anaconda. You should see the Anaconda Prompt under Apps. (You should see something similar to what is shown in Figure 1-6.)

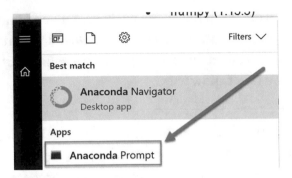

Figure 1-6. *If you type Anaconda in the Start menu search field in Windows 10 you should see at least two entries: the Anaconda Navigator and the Anaconda Prompt.*

Start the Anaconda Prompt (see Figure 1-7). A command-line interface should start. The difference between this and the simple cmd.exe command prompt is that, here, all the Anaconda commands are recognized without having to set up Windows environment variables.

Figure 1-7. *This is what you should see when you start the Anaconda Prompt. Note that the username will be different. You will not see "umber" (my username), but your username.*

Then just type the following commands:

```
conda create -n tensorflow tensorflow
conda activate tensorflow
```

The first line creates an environment called `tensorflow` with TensorFlow already installed, and the second line activates the environment. Then you only need to install the following packages with this code:

```
conda install Jupyter
conda install matplotlib
conda install scikit-learn
```

Note that sometimes you may get some warnings simply by importing TensorFlow with this command:

```
import tensorflow as tf
```

The warnings are due, most probably, by an outdated `hdf5` version. To solve this issue (if it happens to you), try to update it using this code (if you don't get any warning you can skip this step):

```
conda update hdf5
```

You should be all set up. If you have a compatible GPU graphic card installed locally, you can simply install the GPU version of TensorFlow by using this command:

```
conda create -n tensorflow_gpuenv tensorflow-gpu
```

This will create an environment with the GPU version of TensorFlow installed. If you do this, remember to activate the environment and then install all the additional packages as we have done here, in this new environment. Note that to use a GPU, you need additional libraries installed on your system. You can find all the necessary information for the different operating systems (Windows, Mac, and Linux) at `https://www.tensorflow.org/install/gpu`. Note that the TensorFlow website suggests using a Docker image (discussed later in the chapter) if you're using a GPU for hardware acceleration.

Local Jupyter Notebooks

The last step to be able to type code and let it run is to use a Jupyter Notebook from a local installation. The Jupyter Notebook can be described (according to the official website) as follows:

> *The Jupyter Notebook is an open source web application that allows you to create and share documents that contain live code, equations, visualizations, and narrative text. Uses include data cleaning and transformation, numerical simulation, statistical modeling, data visualization, machine learning, and much more.*

It is widely used in the machine learning community and is a good idea to learn how to use it. Check out the Jupyter project website at `http://Jupyter.org/`. It is very instructive and includes many examples of what is possible.

All the code you find in this book has been developed and tested using Jupyter Notebooks. I assume that you have some experience with this web-based development environment. If you need a refresher, I suggest you check out the documentation. You can find it on the Jupyter project website at this address: `http://Jupyter.org/documentation.html`.

To start a notebook in your new environment, you must go back to Anaconda Navigator and click on the triangle to the right of your `tensorflow` environment (if you used a different name, you have to click on the triangle to the right of your new environment), as shown in Figure 1-8. Then click on the Open with Jupyter Notebook option.

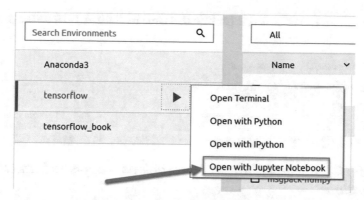

Figure 1-8. *To start a Jupyter Notebook in your new environment, click on the triangle to the right of the TensorFlow environment name and choose Open with Jupyter Notebook*

Your browser starts with a list of the folders in your user folder. (If you are using Windows, this is usually located in c:\Users\<YOUR USER NAME>, where you substitute <YOUR USER NAME> with your username.) From there, you should navigate to a folder where you want to save your notebook files. You can create a new one by clicking on the New button, as illustrated in Figure 1-9.

Figure 1-9. *To create a new notebook, click on the New button located on the top-right part of the page and choose Python 3*

A new page that should look like the one in Figure 1-10 will open.

Figure 1-10. *An empty Jupyter Notebook as it appears immediately after creation*

For example, you can type the following code in the first "cell" (the rectangular space where you can type).

```
a=1
b=2
print(a+b)
```

To evaluate the code press Shift+Enter and you should see the result (3) immediately, as shown in Figure 1-11.

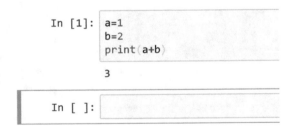

Figure 1-11. *After typing some code in the cell, pressing Shift+Enter evaluates the code in the cell*

The result of a+b is 3 (as shown in Figure 1-11). A new empty cell is automatically created after the result for you to type in.

For more information on how to add comments, equations, inline plots, and much more, I suggest you visit the Jupyter website and check out their documentation.

Note   In case you forget which folder your notebook is in, you can check the URL of the page. For example, in my case, I have `http://localhost:8888/notebooks/Documents/Data%20Science/Projects/Applied%20advanced%20deep%20learning%20(book)/chapter%201/AADL%20-%20Chapter%201%20-%20Introduction.ipynb`. Note that the URL is merely a concatenation of the folders showing where the notebook is located, separated by forward slashes. A %20 character indicates a space. In this case, my notebook is in the `Documents/Data Science/Projects/...` folder. I often work with several notebooks at the same time and it's useful to know where each notebook is located, in case you forget (as I often do).

Benefits and Drawbacks to Anaconda

Let's take a look at the positive and the negative sides of Anaconda now.

Positives:

- The system does not require an active Internet connection (except when installing), so you can work with it everywhere (on the train, for example).

- If you are working on sensitive data that you cannot upload to a cloud service, this is the solution for you, since you can work with data locally.

- You can keep close control over which packages you install and on which environment you create.

Negatives:

- It is quite annoying to get the TensorFlow GPU version to work (you need additional libraries for it to work) with this method. The TensorFlow website suggests using a Docker image (see the next section) for it.

- It is complicated to share your work with other people directly. If sharing is essential, you should consider Google Colab.

- If you are using a corporate laptop that must work behind a firewall or a proxy, it's challenging to work with Jupyter Notebooks, since sometimes, the notebooks may need to connect to the Internet and, if you are behind a firewall, this may not be possible. Installing packages may also be complicated in this case.

- The performance of your code depends on the power and memory of your laptop or desktop. If you are using a slow or old machine, your code may be very slow. In this case, Google Colab may be the better option.

Docker Image

The third option you have is to use a Docker image with TensorFlow installed. Docker (`https://www.docker.com/`) in a way is a bit like a virtual machine. However, unlike a virtual machine, rather than creating a whole virtual operating system, it merely adds components that are not present on the host machine.[5] First, you need to download Docker for your system. A good starting point to learn about it and download it is at `https://docs.docker.com/install/`.

---

[5]`https://opensource.com/resources/what-docker` [Last accessed: 19/12/2018]

First, install Docker on your system. Once you have done so, you can access all different types of TensorFlow versions by using the following command. You must type this command into a command-line interface (for example, cmd in Windows, Terminal on the Mac, or a shell under Linux):

```
docker pull TensorFlow/TensorFlow:<TAG>
```

You should substitute <TAG> with the right text (called a tag as you may imagine), like latest-py3, if you want the latest stable CPU-based build from Python 3.5. You can find an updated list of all tags at https://hub. docker.com/r/TensorFlow/TensorFlow/tags/.

In this example, you would need to type:

```
docker pull tensorflow/tensorflow:latest-py3
```

This command downloads the right image automatically. Docker is efficient, and you can ask it to run the image immediately. If it does not find it locally, it downloads it. You can use the following command to start the image:

```
docker run -it -p 8888:8888 tensorflow/tensorflow:latest-py3
```

If you haven't already downloaded it, this command downloads the latest TensorFlow version based on Python 3 and starts it. You should see output like the following if everything goes well:

```
C:\Users\umber>docker run -it -p 8888:8888 tensorflow/
tensorflow:latest-py3
Unable to find image 'TensorFlow/TensorFlow:latest-py3' locally
latest-py3: Pulling from TensorFlow/TensorFlow
18d680d61657: Already exists
0addb6fece63: Already exists
78e58219b215: Already exists
eb6959a66df2: Already exists
3b57572cd8ae: Pull complete
```

```
56ffb7bbb1f1: Pull complete
1766f64e236d: Pull complete
983abc49e91e: Pull complete
a6f427d2463d: Pull complete
1d2078adb47a: Pull complete
f644ce975673: Pull complete
a4eaf7b16108: Pull complete
8f591b09babe: Pull complete
Digest: sha256:1658b00f06cdf8316cd8a905391235dad4bf25a488f1ea98
9a98a9fe9ec0386e
Status: Downloaded newer image for TensorFlow/TensorFlow:latest-py3
[I 08:53:35.084 NotebookApp] Writing notebook server cookie
secret to /root/.local/share/Jupyter/runtime/notebook_cookie_
secret
[I 08:53:35.112 NotebookApp] Serving notebooks from local
directory: /notebooks
[I 08:53:35.112 NotebookApp] The Jupyter Notebook is running at:
[I 08:53:35.112 NotebookApp] http://(9a30b4f7646e or
127.0.0.1):8888/?token=f2ff836cccb1d688f4d9ad8c7ac3af80011f11ea
77edc425
[I 08:53:35.112 NotebookApp] Use Control-C to stop this server
and shut down all kernels (twice to skip confirmation).
[C 08:53:35.113 NotebookApp]

    Copy/paste this URL into your browser when you connect for
    the first time, to login with a token:
        http://(9a30b4f7646e or 127.0.0.1):8888/?token=f2ff836c
        ccb1d688f4d9ad8c7ac3af80011f11ea77edc425
```

At this point, you can simply connect to a Jupyter server running from the Docker image.

At the end of all previous messages, you'll find the URL you should type in the browser to use Jupyter Notebooks. When you copy the URL, simply substitute *cbc82bb4e78c or 127.0.0.1* with 127.0.0.1. Copy it into the URL field of your browser. The page should look like the one shown in Figure 1-12.

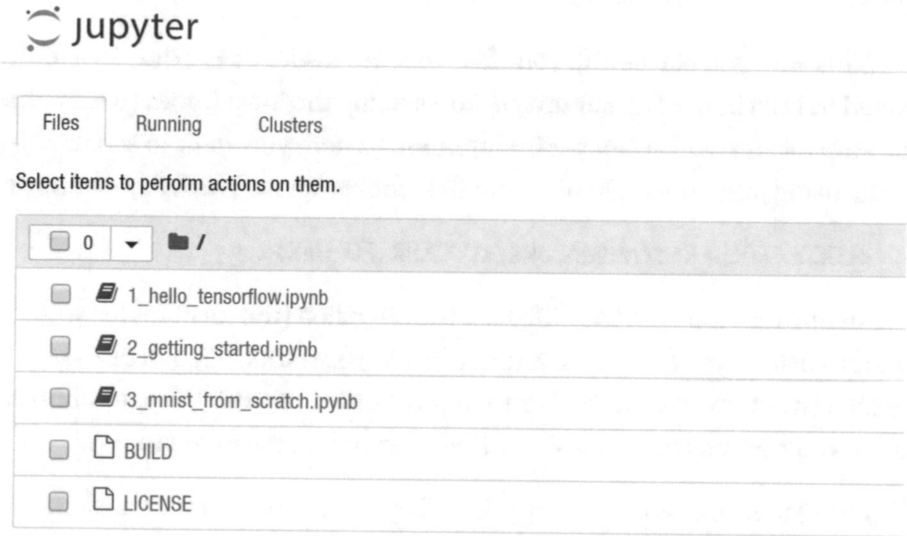

Figure 1-12. *The navigation window you see when using a Docker image Jupyter instance*

It's important to note that if you use the notebook out of the box, all files and notebooks that you create will disappear the next time you start the Docker image.

Note   If you use the Jupyter Notebook server as it is, and you create new notebooks and files, they will all disappear the next time you start the server. You need to mount a local directory that resides on your machine so that you can save your files locally and not in the image itself.

Let's suppose you are using a Windows machine and that your notebooks reside locally at c:\python. To see and use them while using Jupyter Notebooks from the Docker image, you need to start the Docker instance using the -v option in the following way:

```
docker run -it -v c:/python:/notebooks/python -p 8888:8888
TensorFlow/TensorFlow:latest-py3
```

This way, you can see all your files that are under c:\python in a folder called python in the Docker image. You specify the local folder (where the files are local) and the Docker folder name (where you want to see the files while using Jupyter Notebooks from the Docker image) with the -v option:

```
-v <LOCAL FOLDER>:/notebooks/<DOCKER FOLDER>
```

In our example, <LOCAL FOLDER> is c:/python (the local folder you want to use for your locally saved notebooks) and <DOCKER FOLDER> is python (where you want Docker to mount the folder with your notebooks). Once you run the code, you should see output like the following:

```
[I 09:23:49.182 NotebookApp] Writing notebook server cookie
secret to /root/.local/share/Jupyter/runtime/notebook_cookie_
secret
[I 09:23:49.203 NotebookApp] Serving notebooks from local
directory: /notebooks
[I 09:23:49.203 NotebookApp] The Jupyter Notebook is running at:
[I 09:23:49.203 NotebookApp] http://(93d95a95358a or
127.0.0.1):8888/?token=d564b4b1e806c62560ef9e477bfad99245bf9670
52bebf68
[I 09:23:49.203 NotebookApp] Use Control-C to stop this server
and shut down all kernels (twice to skip confirmation).
[C 09:23:49.204 NotebookApp]
```

```
Copy/paste this URL into your browser when you connect for
the first time, to log in with a token:
    http://(93d95a95358a or 127.0.0.1):8888/?token=d564b4b1
    e806c62560ef9e477bfad99245bf967052bebf68
```

Now, when you start your browser with the URL given at the end of
the last message (where you must substitute *93d95a95358a or 127.0.0.1*
with 127.0.0.1), you should see a Python folder named python, as shown
in the one circled in Figure 1-13.

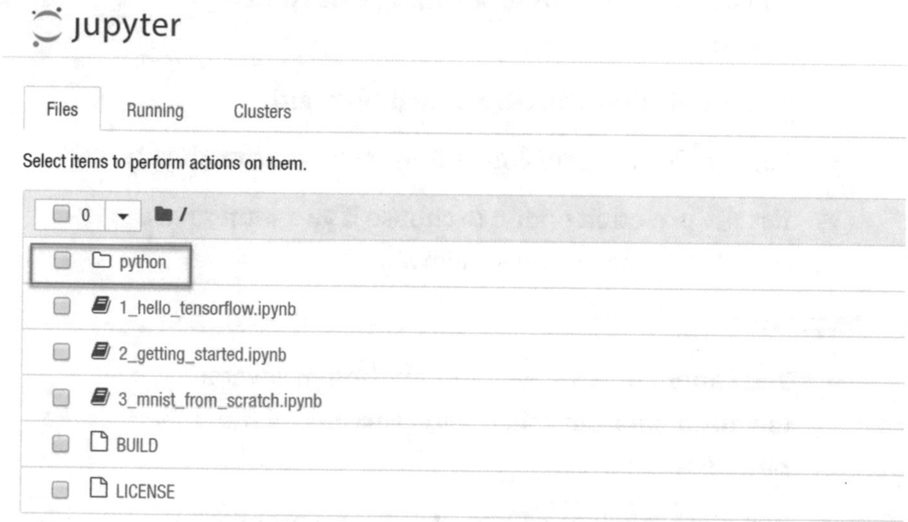

Figure 1-13. *The folder that you should see when starting the Docker
image with the correct -v option. In the folder, you can now see all the
files that are saved locally in the c:\python folder.*

You can now see all your locally saved notebooks, and if you save a
notebook in the folder, you will find it again when you restart your Docker
image.

On a final note, if you have a compatible GPU at your disposal,[6] you can directly download the latest GPU TensorFlow version, for example, using the tag, `latest-gpu`. You can find more information at `https://www.TensorFlow.org/install/gpu`.

Benefits and Drawbacks to a Docker Image

Let's take a look at the positive and the negative aspects of this option.

Positives:

- You don't need to install anything locally, except Docker.

- The installation process is straightforward.

- You get the latest version of TensorFlow automatically.

- It is the preferred option to choose if you want to use the GPU version of TensorFlow.

Negatives:

- You cannot develop with this method in several environments and with several versions of the packages.

- Installing specific package versions is complicated.

- Sharing notebooks is more complicated than with other options.

- The performance of your code is limited by the hardware on which you are running the Docker image.

---

[6]You can find a list of all compatible GPUs at `https://developer.nvidia.com/cuda-gpus` and TensorFlow information at `https://www.TensorFlow.org/install/gpu`.

Which Option Should You Choose?

You can quickly start with any of the options described and later continue with another one. Your code will continue to work. The only thing you need to be aware of is that, if you develop extensive amounts of code with GPU support and then try to run this on a system without GPU support, you may need to modify the code extensively. To decide which option is the best one for you, I provided the following questions and answers.

- **Do you need to work on sensitive data?**

  If you need to work on sensitive data (for example, medical data) that you cannot upload on a cloud service, you should choose a local installation with Anaconda or Docker. You cannot use Google Colab.

- **Do you often work in an environment without an Internet connection?**

  If you want to write code and train your models without an active Internet connection (for example, while commuting), you should choose a local installation of Anaconda or Docker, since Google Colab requires an active Internet connection.

- **Do you need to work on the same notebook in parallel with other people?**

  If you want to share your work with others and work on it at the same time as others, the best solution is to use Google Colab, since it offers a great sharing experience, one that is missing from the local installation options.

- **You don't want to (or can't) install anything on your laptop/desktop?**

  If you don't want to or can't install anything on your laptop or desktop (maybe it's a corporate laptop), you should use Google Colab. You only need an Internet connection and a browser. Keep in mind that some features work only with Google Chrome and not Internet Explorer.

Note   The easiest way to get up and running and start developing models with TensorFlow is probably to use Google Colab since it does not require any installation. Directly go the website, log in, and start writing code. If you need to work locally, the Docker option is probably the easiest solution. It is straightforward to get it up and running and you get to work with the latest version of TensorFlow. If you need the flexibility of many environments and precise control over which version of each package you're using, your only solution is to perform a complete local installation of a Python development environment, like Anaconda.

CHAPTER 2

TensorFlow: Advanced Topics

The TensorFlow library has come a long way from its first appearance. Especially in the last year, many more features have become available that can make the life of researchers a lot easier. Things like eager execution and Keras allow scientists to test and experiment much faster and debug models in ways that were not possible before. It is essential for any researcher to know those methods and know when it makes sense to use them. In this chapter, we will look at few of them: eager execution, GPU acceleration, Keras, how to freeze parts of a network and train only specific parts (used very often, especially in transfer learning and image recognition), and finally how to save and restore models already trained. Those technical skills will be very useful, not only to study this book, but in real-life research projects.

The goal of this chapter is not to teach you how to use Keras from the ground up, or to teach you all the intricacies of the methods, but to show you some advanced techniques to solve some specific problems. Consider the different sections as hints. Remember that is always a good idea to study the official documentation, since methods and functions change very often. In this chapter, I will avoid copying the official documentation, and instead give you few advanced examples of techniques that are very useful and are used very often. To go deeper (pun intended), you should study the official TensorFlow documentation at `https://www.tensorflow.org/`.

© Umberto Michelucci 2019
U. Michelucci, *Advanced Applied Deep Learning*,
https://doi.org/10.1007/978-1-4842-4976-5_2

27

To study and understand advanced topics, a good basis in Tensorflow and Keras is required. A very good resource to get up to speed with Keras is the book *Learn Keras for Deep Neural Networks - A Fast-Track Approach to Modern Deep Learning with Python* from Jojo John Moolayil (https://goo.gl/mW4Ubg). If you don't have much experience, I suggest you get this book and study it before starting this one.

Tensorflow Eager Execution

TensorFlow's eager execution is an imperative programming environment.[1] That, loosely explained, means that the commands are evaluated immediately. That also means that a computational graph is built in the background without you noticing it. Operations return concrete values immediately instead of having first open a session, and then run it. This makes it very easy to start with TensorFlow, since it resembles classical Python programming. Eager execution provides the following advantages:

- Easier debugging: You can debug your models with classical Python debugging tools for immediate checks

- Intuitive interface: You can structure your code naturally, as you would do in a classical Python program

- Support for GPU acceleration is available

To be able to use this execution mode, you will need the latest version of TensorFlow. If you have not yet installed it, see Chapter 1 to learn how to do it.

---

[1]https://www.tensorflow.org/guide/eager (accessed 17th January, 2019)

Enabling Eager Execution

To enable eager execution, you can use the following code:

```
import tensorflow as tf
tf.enable_eager_execution()
```

Remember that you need to do that right at the beginning, after the `imports` and before any other command. Otherwise, you will get an error message. If that is the case, you can simply restart the kernel of the notebook.

For example, you can easily add two tensors

```
print(tf.add(1, 2))
```

and get immediately this result

```
tf.Tensor(3, shape=(), dtype=int32)
```

If you don't enable eager execution and try the `print` command again, you will get this result

```
Tensor("Add:0", shape=(), dtype=int32)
```

Since TensorFlow has not yet evaluated the node. You would need the following code to get the result:

```
sess = tf.Session()
print(sess.run(tf.add(1,2)))
sess.close()
```

The result will be, of course, 3. This second version of the code creates a graph, then opens a session, and then evaluates it. With eager you get the result immediately. You can easily check if you have enabled eager execution with this:

```
tf.executing_eagerly()
```

It should return `True` or `False`, depending on if you have enabled it or not.

Polynomial Fitting with Eager Execution

Let's check how eager execution works in a practical example.[2]

Keep in mind you need the following imports:

```
import tensorflow as tf
import numpy as np
import matplotlib.pyplot as plt
import tensorflow.contrib.eager as tfe
tf.enable_eager_execution()
```

Let's generate some fake data for this function

$$y = x^3 - 4x^2 - 2x + 2$$

with the code

```
x = np.arange(0, 5, 0.1)
y = x**3 - 4*x**2 - 2*x + 2
y_noise = y + np.random.normal(0, 1.5, size=(len(x),))
```

We have created two numpy arrays: y, which contains the function evaluated over the array x, and y_noise, which contains y with some noise added. You can see how the data looks in Figure 2-1.

---

[2]You can find the notebook with the code in the book repository. To find it, go to the Apress book website and click on the Download Code button. The link points to the GitHub repository. The notebook is in the Chapter2 folder.

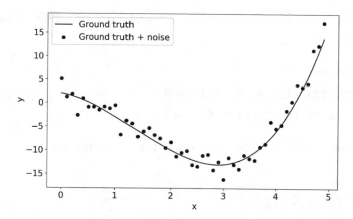

Figure 2-1. *The plot shows the two numpy arrays y (ground truth) and y_noise (ground truth + noise)*

Now we need to define a model that we want to fit and define our loss function (the one we want to minimize with TensorFlow). Remember we are facing a regression problem, so we will use the Mean Squared Error (MSE) as our loss function. The functions we need are as follows:

```
class Model(object):
  def __init__(self):
    self.w = tfe.Variable(tf.random_normal([4])) # The 4
    parameters

  def f(self, x):
    return self.w[0] * x ** 3 + self.w[1] * x ** 2 +
    self.w[2] * x + self.w[3]
```

and

```
def loss(model, x, y):
    err = model.f(x) - y
    return tf.reduce_mean(tf.square(err))
```

Now is easy to minimize the loss function. First let's define some variables we will need:

```
model = Model()
grad = tfe.implicit_gradients(loss)
optimizer = tf.train.AdamOptimizer()
```

Then let's, with a for loop, minimize the loss function:

```
iters = 20000
for i in range(iters):
  optimizer.apply_gradients(grad(model, x, y))
  if i % 1000 == 0:
        print("Iteration {}, loss: {}".format(i+1, loss(model,
        x, y).numpy()))
```

This code will produce some outputs showing you the value for the loss function each 1,000 iterations. Note that we are feeding all the data in one batch to the optimizer (since we have only 50 data points, we don't really need to use mini-batches).

You should see several output lines like this one:

```
Iteration 20000, loss: 0.004939439240843058
```

The loss function plot versus the number of the iterations can be seen in Figure 2-2 and is decreasing constantly, as expected.

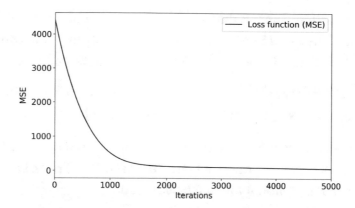

Figure 2-2. *The loss function (MSE) vs. the iteration number is decreasing as expected. That shows clearly that the optimizer is doing a good job finding the best weights to minimize the loss function.*

In Figure 2-3, you can see the function the optimizer was able to find, by minimizing the weights.

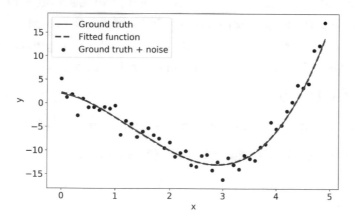

Figure 2-3. *The red dashed line is the function obtained by minimizing the loss function with the Adam optimizer. The method worked perfectly and found the right function efficiently.*

What you should note is that we did not create a computational graph explicitly and then evaluate it in a session. We simply used the commands as we would with any Python code. For example, in the code

```
for i in range(iters):
  optimizer.apply_gradients(grad(model, x, y))
```

we simply call a TensorFlow operation in a loop without the need of a session. With eager execution, it's easy to start using TensorFlow operations quickly without too much overhead.

MNIST Classification with Eager Execution

To give another example of how you can build a model with eager execution, let's build a classifier for the famous MNIST dataset. This is a dataset containing 60000 images of handwritten digits (from 0 to 9), each with a dimension of 28x28 in gray levels (each pixel has a value ranging from 0 to 255). If you have not seen the MNIST dataset, I suggest you check out the original website at https://goo.gl/yF0yH, where you will find all the information. We will implement the following steps:

- Load the dataset.

- Normalize the features and one-hot encode the labels.

- Convert the data in a tf.data.Dataset object.

- Build a Keras model with two layers, each with 1024 neurons.

- Define the optimizer and the loss function.

- Minimize the loss function using the gradients and the optimizer directly.

Let's start.

While following the code, note how we implement each piece as we would do with plain numpy, meaning without the need of creating a graph or opening a TensorFlow session.

So first let's load the MNIST dataset using the keras.datasets.mnist package, reshape it, and one-hot encode the labels.

```python
import tensorflow as tf
import tensorflow.keras as keras

num_classes = 10

mnist = tf.keras.datasets.mnist
(x_train, y_train), (x_test, y_test) = mnist.load_data()

image_vector_size = 28*28
x_train = x_train.reshape(x_train.shape[0], image_vector_size)
x_test = x_test.reshape(x_test.shape[0], image_vector_size)

y_train = keras.utils.to_categorical(y_train, num_classes)
y_test = keras.utils.to_categorical(y_test, num_classes)
```

Then let's convert the arrays in a tf.data.Dataset object. In case you don't understand what this is, don't worry, we will look at this more later in this chapter. For the moment, it suffices to know that it is a convenient way to use mini-batches while you train your network.

```python
dataset = tf.data.Dataset.from_tensor_slices(
    (tf.cast(x_train/255.0, tf.float32),
     tf.cast(y_train,tf.int64)))

dataset = dataset.shuffle(60000).batch(64)
```

Now let's build the model using a feed-forward neural network with two layers, each with 1024 neurons:

```
mnist_model = tf.keras.Sequential([
  tf.keras.layers.Dense(1024, input_shape=(784,)),
  tf.keras.layers.Dense(1024),
  tf.keras.layers.Dense(10)
])
```

Up to now we have not done anything particularly new, so you should be able to follow what we did quite easily. The next step is to define the optimizer (we will use Adam) and the list that will contain the loss function history:

```
optimizer = tf.train.AdamOptimizer()
loss_history = []
```

At this point we can start with the actual training. We will have two nested loops—the first is for the epochs, the second for the batches.

```
for i in range(10): # Epochs
  print ("\nEpoch:", i)
  for (batch, (images, labels)) in enumerate(dataset.
  take(60000)):
    if batch % 100 == 0:
      print('.', end="")
    with tf.GradientTape() as tape:
      logits = mnist_model(images, training=True) # Prediction
      of the model
      loss_value = tf.losses.sparse_softmax_cross_entropy(tf.
      argmax(labels, axis = 1), logits)

      loss_history.append(loss_value.numpy())
      grads = tape.gradient(loss_value, mnist_model.variables)
      # Evaluation of gradients
```

```
optimizer.apply_gradients(zip(grads, mnist_model.
variables),
                              global_step=tf.train.get_or_
                              create_global_step())
```

The part of the code that is probably new to you is the part that contains these two lines:

```
grads = tape.gradient(loss_value, mnist_model.variables)
optimizer.apply_gradients(zip(grads, mnist_model.variables),
                              global_step=tf.train.get_or_
                              create_global_step())
```

The first line calculates the gradients of the loss_value TensorFlow operation with respect to the mnist_model.variables (the weights basically), and the second line uses the gradients to let the optimizer update the weights. To understand how Keras evaluates gradients automatically, I suggest you check the official documentation at https:// goo.gl/s9Uqjc. Running the code will finally train the network. As the training progress, you should see output like this for each epoch:

```
Epoch: 0
. . . . . . . . . .
```

Now to check the accuracy, you can simply run the following two lines (that should be self-explanatory):

```
probs = tf.nn.softmax(mnist_model(x_train))
print(tf.reduce_mean(tf.cast(tf.equal(tf.argmax(probs, axis=1),
tf.argmax(y_train, axis = 1)), tf.float32)))
```

This will give you as a result a tensor that will contain the accuracy reached by the model:

```
tf.Tensor(0.8980333, shape=(), dtype=float32)
```

In this example, we reached 89.8% accuracy, a relatively good result for such a simple network. Of course, you could try to train the model for more epochs or try to change the learning rate, for example. In case you are wondering where we defined the learning rate, we did not. When we define the optimizer as `tf.train.AdamOptimizer`, TensorFlow will use, if not specified differently, the standard value of 10^{-3}. You can check this by looking at the documentation at `https://goo.gl/pU7yrB`.

We could check one prediction easily. Let's get one image from our dataset:

```
image = x_train[4:5,:]
label = y_train[4]
```

If we plot the image, we will see the number nine (see Figure 2-4).

Figure 2-4. *One image from the MNIST dataset. This happens to be a 9.*

We can easily check what the model predicts:

```
print(tf.argmax(tf.nn.softmax(mnist_model(image)), axis = 1))
```

This returns the following, as we expected:

```
tf.Tensor([9], shape=(1,), dtype=int64)
```

You should note how we wrote the code. We did not create a graph explicitly, but we simply used functions and operations as we would have done with numpy. There is no need to think in graphs and sessions. This is how eager execution works.

TensorFlow and Numpy Compatibility

TensorFlow makes switching to and from numpy arrays very easy:

- TensorFlow converts numpy arrays to tensors

- Numpy converts tensors to numpy arrays

Converting a tensor to a numpy array is very easy and is enough to invoke the .numpy() method. This operation is fast and cheap since the numpy array and the tensor share the memory, so no shifting around in memory is happening. Now this is not possible if you are using GPU hardware acceleration, since numpy arrays cannot be stored in GPU memory and tensors can. Converting will involve copying data from the GPU memory to the CPU memory. Simply something to keep in mind.

Note   Typically, TensorFlow tensors and numpy arrays share the same memory. Converting one to another is a very cheap operation. But if you use GPU accelerations, tensors may be held in the GPU memory, and numpy arrays cannot, so copying data will be required. This may be more expensive in terms of running time.

Hardware Acceleration

Checking the Availability of the GPU

It is worth it to show briefly how to use GPUs and what difference it may make, just to give you a feeling for it. If you have never seen it, it's quite impressive. The easiest way to test GPU acceleration is to use Google Colab. Create a new notebook in Google Colab, activate GPU[3] acceleration, and import TensorFlow as usual:

```
import tensorflow as tf
```

Then we need to test if we have a GPU at our disposal. This can be easily done with this code:

```
print(tf.test.is_gpu_available())
```

This will return True or False depending on if a GPU is available. In a slightly more sophisticated way, it can be done in this way:

```
device_name = tf.test.gpu_device_name()
if device_name != '/device:GPU:0':
  raise SystemError('GPU device not found.')
print('Found GPU at: {}'.format(device_name))
```

If you run the code, you may get this error:

```
SystemErrorTraceback (most recent call last)
<ipython-input-1-d1680108c58e> in <module>()
      2 device_name = tf.test.gpu_device_name()
      3 if device_name != '/device:GPU:0':
```

---

[3]You can find this article at https://goo.gl/hXKNnf to learn how to do it.

40

```
----> 4   raise SystemError('GPU device not found')
      5 print('Found GPU at: {}'.format(device_name))
SystemError: GPU device not found
```

The reason is that you may have not yet configured the notebook (if you are in Google Colab) to use a GPU. Or, if you are working on a laptop or desktop, you may have not installed the right TensorFlow version or you may not have a compatible GPU available.

To enable the GPU hardware acceleration in Google Colab, choose the Edit ➤ Notebook Settings menu option. You are then presented with a window where you can set up the hardware accelerator. By default, it is set to None. If you set it to GPU and run the previous code again, you should get this message:

```
Found GPU at: /device:GPU:0
```

Device Names

Note how the device name, in our case /device:GPU:0, encodes lots of information. This name ends with GPU:<NUMBER>, where <NUMBER> is an integer that can be as big as the number of GPUs you have at your disposal. You can get a list of all the devices you have at your disposal with this code:

```
local_device_protos = device_lib.list_local_devices()
print(local_device_protos)
```

You will get a list of all the devices. Each list entry will resemble this one (this example refers to a GPU device):

```
name: "/device:XLA_GPU:0"
device_type: "XLA_GPU"
memory_limit: 17179869184
locality {
}
```

```
incarnation: 16797530695469281809
physical_device_desc: "device: XLA_GPU device"
```

With a function like this one:

```
def get_available_gpus():
    local_device_protos = device_lib.list_local_devices()
    return [x.name for x in local_device_protos if x.device_
    type.endswith('GPU')]
```

You will get an easier-to-read result like this one[4]:

```
['/device:XLA_GPU:0', '/device:GPU:0']
```

Explicit Device Placement

It is very easy to place an operation on a specific device. That can be achieved using the tf.device context. For example, to place an operation on a CPU, you can use the following code:

```
with tf.device("/cpu:0"):
    # SOME OPERATION
```

Or to place an operation on a GPU, you can use the code:

```
with tf.device('/gpu:0'):
    # SOME OPERATION
```

Note   Unless explicitly declared, TensorFlow automatically decides on which device each operation must run. Don't assume that if you don't specify the device explicitly that your code will run on a CPU.

---

[4]The result was obtained when calling the function in a Google Colab notebook.

GPU Acceleration Demonstration: Matrix Multiplication

It is interesting to see what effect hardware acceleration may have. To learn more about using GPUs, it is instructive to read the official documentation, which can be found at `https://www.TensorFlow.org/guide/using_gpu`.

Start with the following code[5]:

```
config = tf.ConfigProto()
config.gpu_options.allow_growth = True
sess = tf.Session(config=config)
```

The second line is needed since TensorFlow starts to allocate a little GPU memory. As the session is started and the processes run, more GPU memory is then allocated as needed. Then a session is created. Let's try to multiply two matrices of dimensions 10000x10000 filled with random values and see if using a GPU makes a difference. The following code will run the multiplication on a GPU:

```
%%time
with tf.device('/gpu:0'):
  tensor1 = tf.random_normal((10000, 10000))
  tensor2 = tf.random_normal((10000, 10000))
  prod = tf.linalg.matmul(tensor1, tensor2)
  prod_sum = tf.reduce_sum(prod)

  sess.run(prod_sum)
```

And the following runs it on a CPU:

```
%%time
with tf.device('/cpu:0'):
```

---

[5]The code has been inspired by the Google code in the Google Colab documentation.

```
tensor1 = tf.random_normal((10000, 10000))
tensor2 = tf.random_normal((10000, 10000))
prod = tf.linalg.matmul(tensor1, tensor2)
prod_sum = tf.reduce_sum(prod)

sess.run(prod_sum)
```

When I ran the code, I got 1.86 sec total time on a GPU and 1min 4sec on a CPU: a factor 32 times faster. You can imagine then, when doing such calculations over and over (as is often the case in deep learning), that you'll get quite a performance boost in your evaluations. Using TPUs is slightly more complicated and goes beyond the scope of this book, so we will skip that.

Note   Using a GPU does not always give you a performance boost. When the tensors involved are small, you will not see a huge difference between using a GPU and a CPU. The real difference will become evident when the dimensions of the tensors start to grow.

If you try to run the same code on smaller tensors, for example 100x100, you will not see any difference at all between using a GPU and a CPU. The tensors are small enough that a CPU will get the result as fast as a GPU. For two 100x100 matrices, GPU and CPU both give a result in roughly 20ms. Typically, practitioners let CPUs do all the preprocessing (for example, normalization, loading of data, etc.) and then let GPUs perform all the big tensor operations during training.

Note   Typically, you should evaluate only expensive tensor operations (like matrix multiplications or convolution) on GPUs and do all preprocessing (like data loading, cleaning, etc.) on a CPU.

We will see later in the book (where applicable) how to do that. But don't be afraid. You will be able to use the code and follow the examples without a GPU at your disposal.

Effect of GPU Acceleration on the MNIST Example

It is instructive to see the effect of hardware acceleration on the MNIST example. To run the training of the model completely on the CPU we need to force TensorFlow to do it, since otherwise it will try to place expensive operations on a GPU when available. To do that, you can use this code:

```
with tf.device('/cpu:0'):
  for i in range(10): # Loop for the Epochs
    print ("\nEpoch:", i)
    for (batch, (images, labels)) in enumerate(dataset.
    take(60000)): # Loop for the mini-batches
      if batch % 100 == 0:
        print('.', end="")
      with tf.GradientTape() as tape:
        logits = mnist_model(images, training=True)
        loss_value = tf.losses.sparse_softmax_cross_entropy(tf.
        argmax(labels, axis = 1), logits)

        loss_history.append(loss_value.numpy())
        grads = tape.gradient(loss_value, mnist_model.
        variables)
        optimizer.apply_gradients(zip(grads, mnist_model.
        variables),

                                        global_step=tf.train.get_or_
                                        create_global_step())
```

This code, on Google Colab, runs in roughly 8 minutes and 41 seconds. If we put all the possible operations on a GPU, using this code:

```
for i in range(10): # Loop for the Epochs
  print ("\nEpoch:", i)

  for (batch, (images, labels)) in enumerate(dataset.
  take(60000)): # Loop for the mini-batches
    if batch % 100 == 0:
      print('.', end=")
    labels = tf.cast(labels, dtype = tf.int64)

    with tf.GradientTape() as tape:

      with tf.device('/gpu:0'):
        logits = mnist_model(images, training=True)

      with tf.device('/cpu:0'):
        tgmax = tf.argmax(labels, axis = 1, output_type=tf.
        int64)

      with tf.device('/gpu:0'):
        loss_value = tf.losses.sparse_softmax_cross_
        entropy(tgmax, logits)

        loss_history.append(loss_value.numpy())
        grads = tape.gradient(loss_value, mnist_model.
        variables)
        optimizer.apply_gradients(zip(grads, mnist_model.
        variables),
                                  global_step=tf.train.get_
                                  or_create_global_step())
```

It will run in 1 minute and 24 seconds. The reason that the `tf.argmax()` has been placed on a CPU is that at the time of writing the GPU implementation of `tf.argmax` has a bug and does not work as intended.

You can clearly see the dramatic effect that GPU acceleration has, even on a simple network like the one we used.

Training Only Specific Layers

You should now know that Keras works with layers. When you define one, let's say a Dense layer, as follows:

```
layer1 = Dense(32)
```

You can pass a `trainable` argument (that is Boolean) to a layer constructor. This will stop the optimizer to update its weights

```
layer1 = dense(32, trainable = False)
```

But this would not be very useful. What is needed is the possibility of changing this property after instantiation. This is easy to do. For example, you can use the following code

```
layer = Dense(32)
# something useful happens here
layer.trainable = False
```

Note   For the trainable property's change to take effect, you need to call the `compile()` method on your model. Otherwise, the change will not have any effect while using the `fit()` method.

Training Only Specific Layers: An Example

To understand better how this all works, let's look at an example. Let's again consider a feed-forward network with two layers:

```
model = Sequential()
model.add(Dense(32, activation='relu', input_dim=784,
name = 'input'))
model.add(Dense(32, activation='relu', name = 'hidden1'))
```

Note how we created a model with two Dense layers with a name property. One is called input and the second is called hidden1. Now you can check the network structure with model.summary(). In this simple example, you will get the following output:

Layer (type)	Output Shape	Param #
input (Dense)	(None, 32)	25120
hidden1 (Dense)	(None, 32)	1056

```
Total params: 26,176
Trainable params: 26,176
Non-trainable params: 0
```

Note how all the parameters are trainable and how you can find the layer name in the first column. Please take note, since assigning each layer a name will be useful in the future. To freeze the layer called hidden1, you simply need to find the layer with the name and change its trainable property as follows:

```
model.get_layer('hidden1').trainable = False
```

Now, if you check the model summary again, you will see a different number of trainable parameters:

Layer (type)	Output Shape	Param #
input (Dense)	(None, 32)	25120
hidden1 (Dense)	(None, 32)	1056

```
Total params: 26,176
Trainable params: 25,120
Non-trainable params: 1,056
```

As you can see, the 1056 parameters contained in the hidden1 layer are no longer trainable. The layer is now frozen. If you have not assigned names to the layers and you want to find out what the layers are called, you can use the model.summary() function or you can simply loop through the layers in the model with this:

```
for layer in model.layers:
  print (layer.name)
```

This code will give you the following output:

```
input
hidden1
```

Note that model.layers is simply a list with layers as elements. As such, you can use the classical way of accessing elements from a list. For example, to access the last layer, you can use:

```
model.layers[-1]
```

Or to access the first layer, use:

```
model.layers[0]
```

To freeze the last layer, for example, you can simply use:

```
model.layers[-1].trainable = False
```

Note   When you change a property of a layer in Keras, like the `trainable` property, remember to recompile the model with the `compile()` function. Otherwise, the change will not take effect during the training.

To summarize, consider the following code[6]:

```
x = Input(shape=(4,))
layer = Dense(8)
layer.trainable = False
y = layer(x)
frozen_model = Model(x, y)
```

Now, if we run the following code:

```
frozen_model.compile(optimizer='Adam', loss='mse')
frozen_model.fit(data, labels)
```

It will not modify the weights of layer. In fact, calling `frozen_model.summary()` gives us this:

---

[6]Check the official documentation for the example at `https://keras.io/getting-started/faq/#how-can-i-freeze-keras-layers`.

Layer (type)	Output Shape	Param #
===		
input_1 (InputLayer)	(None, 4)	0
dense_6 (Dense)	(None, 8)	40
===		
Total params: 40		
Trainable params: 0		
Non-trainable params: 40		

As expected, there are no trainable parameters. We can simply modify the layer.trainable property:

```
layer.trainable = True
trainable_model = Model(x, y)
```

Now we compile and fit the model:

```
trainable_model.compile(optimizer='Adam', loss='mse')
trainable_model.fit(data, labels)
```

This time the weights of layer will be updated. We can check on that with trainable_model.summary():

Layer (type)	Output Shape	Param #
===		
input_1 (InputLayer)	(None, 4)	0
dense_6 (Dense)	(None, 8)	40
===		

```
Total params: 40
Trainable params: 40
Non-trainable params: 0
```

Now all the parameters are trainable, as we wanted.

Removing Layers

It's very useful to remove one or more of the last layers in a model and add different ones to fine-tune it. The idea is used very often in transfer learning, when you train a network and want to fine-tune its behavior by training only the last few layers. Let's consider the following model:

```
model = Sequential()
model.add(Dense(32, activation='relu', input_dim=784, name =
'input'))
model.add(Dense(32, activation='relu', name = 'hidden1'))
model.add(Dense(32, activation='relu', name = 'hidden2'))
```

The summary() call will give this output:

Layer (type)	Output Shape	Param #
input (Dense)	(None, 32)	25120
hidden1 (Dense)	(None, 32)	1056
hidden2 (Dense)	(None, 32)	1056

```
Total params: 27,232
Trainable params: 27,232
Non-trainable params: 0
```

Say you want to build a second model, keeping your trained weights in the input and hidden1 layers, but you want to substitute the hidden2 layer with a different layer (let's say one with 16 neurons). You can easily do that in the following way:

```
model2 = Sequential()
for layer in model.layers[:-1]:
  model2.add(layer)
```

This gives you:

Layer (type)	Output Shape	Param #
input (Dense)	(None, 32)	25120
hidden1 (Dense)	(None, 32)	1056

```
Total params: 26,176
Trainable params: 26,176
Non-trainable params: 0
```

At this point, you can simply add a new layer with the following:

```
model2.add(Dense(16, activation='relu', name = 'hidden3'))
```

It has the following structure:

Layer (type)	Output Shape	Param #
input (Dense)	(None, 32)	25120
hidden1 (Dense)	(None, 32)	1056
hidden3 (Dense)	(None, 16)	528

```
Total params: 26,704
Trainable params: 26,704
Non-trainable params: 0
```

After that, remember to compile your model. For example, for a regression problem, your code may look like this:

```
model.compile(loss='mse', optimizer='Adam', metrics=['mse'])
```

Keras Callback Functions

It is instructive to understand a bit better what Keras callback functions are since they are used quite often while developing models. This is from the official documentation[7]:

> *A callback is a set of functions to be applied at given stages of the training procedure.*

The idea is that you can pass a list of callback functions to the .fit() method of the Sequential or Model classes. Relevant methods of the

---

[7]https://keras.io/callbacks/

callbacks will then be called at each stage of training [`https://keras.io/callbacks/, Accessed 01/02/2019`]. Keunwoo Choi has written a nice overview on how to write a callback class that you can find at `https://goo.gl/hL37wq`. We summarize it here and expand it with some practical examples.

Custom Callback Class

The abstract base class, called `Callback`, can be found at the time of this writing at

`tensorflow/python/keras/callbacks.py` (`https://goo.gl/uMrMbH`).

To start, you need to define a custom class. The main methods you want to redefine are typically the following

- `on_train_begin`: Called at the beginning of training

- `on_train_end`: Called at the end of training

- `on_epoch_begin`: Called at the start of an epoch

- `on_epoch_end`: Called at the end of an epoch

- `on_batch_begin`: Called right before processing a batch

- `on_batch_end`: Called at the end of a batch

This can be done with the following code:

```
import keras
class My_Callback(keras.callbacks.Callback):
    def on_train_begin(self, logs={}):
        return

    def on_train_end(self, logs={}):
        return

    def on_epoch_begin(self, epoch, logs={}):
        return
```

```
def on_epoch_end(self, epoch, logs={}):
    return

def on_batch_begin(self, batch, logs={}):
    return

def on_batch_end(self, batch, logs={}):
    self.losses.append(logs.get('loss'))
    return
```

Each of the methods has slightly different inputs that you may use in your class. Let's look at them briefly (you can find them in the original Python code at https://goo.gl/uMrMbH).

on_epoch_begin, on_epoch_end

Arguments:

> epoch: integer, index of epoch.

> logs: dictionary of logs.

on_train_begin, on_train_end

Arguments:

> logs: dictionary of logs.

on_batch_begin, on_batch_end

Arguments:

> batch: integer, index of batch within the current epoch.

> logs: dictionary of logs.

Let's see with an example of how we can use this class.

Example of a Custom Callback Class

Let's again consider the MNIST example. It's the same code you have seen by now:

```
import tensorflow as tf
from tensorflow import keras
(train_images, train_labels), (test_images, test_labels) =
tf.keras.datasets.mnist.load_data()

train_labels = train_labels[:5000]
test_labels = test_labels[:5000]

train_images = train_images[:5000].reshape(-1, 28 * 28) / 255.0
test_images = test_images[:5000].reshape(-1, 28 * 28) / 255.0
```

Let's define a Sequential model for our example:

```
model = tf.keras.models.Sequential([
    keras.layers.Dense(512, activation=tf.keras.activations.
    relu, input_shape=(784,)),
    keras.layers.Dropout(0.2),
    \keras.layers.Dense(10, activation=tf.keras.activations.
    softmax)
  ])

model.compile(optimizer='adam',
              loss=tf.keras.losses.sparse_categorical_
              crossentropy,
              metrics=['accuracy'])
```

Now let's write a custom callback class, redefining only one of the methods to see the inputs. For example, let's see what the logs variable contains at the beginning of the training:

```
class CustomCallback1(keras.callbacks.Callback):
    def on_train_begin(self, logs={}):
        print (logs)
        return
```

You can then use it with:

```
CC1 = CustomCallback1()
model.fit(train_images, train_labels,  epochs = 2,
          validation_data = (test_images,test_labels),
          callbacks = [CC1])  # pass callback to training
```

Remember to always instantiate the class and pass the CC1 variable, and not the class itself. You will get the following:

```
Train on 5000 samples, validate on 5000 samples
{}
Epoch 1/2
5000/5000 [==============================] - 1s 274us/step -
loss: 0.0976 - acc: 0.9746 - val_loss: 0.2690 - val_acc: 0.9172
Epoch 2/2
5000/5000 [==============================] - 1s 275us/step -
loss: 0.0650 - acc: 0.9852 - val_loss: 0.2925 - val_acc: 0.9114
{}
<tensorflow.python.keras.callbacks.History at 0x7f795d750208>
```

The logs dictionary is empty, as you can see from the {}. Let's expand our class a bit:

```
class CustomCallback2(keras.callbacks.Callback):
    def on_train_begin(self, logs={}):
        print (logs)
        return

    def on_epoch_end(self, epoch, logs={}):
        print ("Just finished epoch", epoch)
        print (logs)
        return
```

Now we train the network with this:

```
CC2 = CustomCallback2()
model.fit(train_images, train_labels,  epochs = 2,
        validation_data = (test_images,test_labels),
        callbacks = [CC2])  # pass callback to training
```

This will give the following output (reported here for just one epoch for brevity):

```
Train on 5000 samples, validate on 5000 samples
{}
Epoch 1/2
4864/5000 [=============================>.] - ETA: 0s - loss:
0.0511 - acc: 0.9879
Just finished epoch 0
{'val_loss': 0.2545496598124504, 'val_acc': 0.9244, 'loss':
0.05098680723309517, 'acc': 0.9878}
```

Now things are starting to get interesting. The logs dictionary now contains a lot more information that we can access and use. In the dictionary, we have val_loss, val_acc, and acc. So let's customize our output a bit. Let's set verbose = 0 in the fit() call to suppress the standard output and then generate our own.

Our new class will be:

```
class CustomCallback3(keras.callbacks.Callback):
    def on_train_begin(self, logs={}):
        print (logs)
        return

    def on_epoch_end(self, epoch, logs={}):
        print ("Just finished epoch", epoch)
        print ('Loss evaluated on the validation dataset
        =',logs.get('val_loss'))
        print ('Accuracy reached is', logs.get('acc'))
        return
```

We can train our network with:

```
CC3 = CustomCallback3()
model.fit(train_images, train_labels,  epochs = 2,
        validation_data = (test_images,test_labels),
        callbacks = [CC3], verbose = 0)  # pass callback to
        training
```

We will get this:

```
{}
Just finished epoch 0
Loss evaluated on the validation dataset = 0.2546206972360611
```

The empty {} simply indicates the empty logs dictionary that on_train_begin received. Of course, you can print information every few epochs. For example, by modifying the on_epoch_end() function as follows:

```
def on_epoch_end(self, epoch, logs={}):
        if (epoch % 10 == 0):
            print ("Just finished epoch", epoch)
```

```
    print ('Loss evaluated on the validation dataset
    =',logs.get('val_loss'))
    print ('Accuracy reached is', logs.get('acc'))
  return
```

You will get the following output if you train your network for 30 epochs:

```
{}
Just finished epoch 0
Loss evaluated on the validation dataset = 0.3692033936366439
Accuracy reached is 0.9932
Just finished epoch 10
Loss evaluated on the validation dataset = 0.3073081444747746
Accuracy reached is 1.0
Just finished epoch 20
Loss evaluated on the validation dataset = 0.31566708440929653
Accuracy reached is 0.9992
<tensorflow.python.keras.callbacks.History at 0x7f796083c4e0>
```

Now you should start to get an idea as to how you can perform several things during the training. A typical use of callbacks that we will look at in the next section is saving your model every few epochs. But you can, for example, save accuracy values in lists to be able to plot them later, or simply plot metrics to see how your training is going.

Save and Load Models

It is often useful to save a model on disk, in order to be able to continue the training at a later stage, or to reuse a previously trained model. To see how you can do this, let's consider the MNIST dataset again for the sake of giving a concrete example.[8] The entire code is available in a dedicated notebook in the book's GitHub repository in the chapter 2 folder.

You will need the following imports:

```
import os
import tensorflow as tf
from tensorflow import keras
```

Again, let's load the MNIST dataset and take the first 5000 observations.

```
(train_images, train_labels), (test_images, test_labels) =
tf.keras.datasets.mnist.load_data()
train_labels = train_labels[:5000]
test_labels = test_labels[:5000]
train_images = train_images[:5000].reshape(-1, 28 * 28) / 255.0
test_images = test_images[:5000].reshape(-1, 28 * 28) / 255.0
```

Then let's build a simple Keras model using a Dense layer with 512 neurons, a bit of dropout, and the classical 10 neuron output layer for classification (remember the MNIST dataset has 10 classes).

```
model = tf.keras.models.Sequential([
    keras.layers.Dense(512, activation=tf.keras.activations.
    relu, input_shape=(784,)),
    keras.layers.Dropout(0.2),
    keras.layers.Dense(10, activation=tf.keras.activations.
    softmax)
  ])

model.compile(optimizer='adam',
```

---

[8]The example was inspired by the official Keras documentation at https://www.tensorflow.org/tutorials/keras/save_and_restore_models.

```
loss=tf.keras.losses.sparse_categorical_
crossentropy,
metrics=['accuracy'])
```

We added a bit of dropout, since this model has 407'050 trainable parameters. You can check this number simply by using `model.summary()`.

What we need to do is define where we want to save the model on the disk. And we can do that (for example) in this way:

```
checkpoint_path = "training/cp.ckpt"
checkpoint_dir = os.path.dirname(checkpoint_path)
```

After that, we need to define a callback (remember what we did in the last section) that will save the weights:

```
cp_callback = tf.keras.callbacks.ModelCheckpoint(checkpoint_path,
                                                 save_weights_
                                                 only=True,
                                                 verbose=1)
```

Note that now we don't need to define a class as we did in the previous section, since `ModelCheckpoint` inherits from the `Callback` class.

Then we can simply train the model, specifying the correct callback function:

```
model.fit(train_images, train_labels,  epochs = 10,
          validation_data = (test_images,test_labels),
          callbacks = [cp_callback])
```

If you run a `!ls` command, you should see at least three files:

- `cp.ckpt.data-00000-of-00001`: Contains the weights (in case the number of weights is large, you will get many files like this one)

- `cp.ckpt.index`: This file indicates which weights are in which files

- `checkpoint`: This text file contains information about the checkpoint itself

We can now test our method. The previous code will give you a model that will reach an accuracy on the validation dataset of roughly 92%. Now if we define a second model as so:

```
model2 = tf.keras.models.Sequential([
    keras.layers.Dense(512, activation=tf.keras.activations.
    relu, input_shape=(784,)),
    keras.layers.Dropout(0.2),
    keras.layers.Dense(10, activation=tf.keras.activations.
    softmax)
  ])
```

```
model2.compile(optimizer='adam',
               loss=tf.keras.losses.sparse_categorical_
               crossentropy,
               metrics=['accuracy'])
```

And we check its accuracy on the validation dataset with this:

```
loss, acc = model2.evaluate(test_images, test_labels)
print("Untrained model, accuracy: {:5.2f}%".format(100*acc))
```

We will get an accuracy of roughly 8.6%. That was expected, since this model has not been trained yet. But now we can load the saved weights in this model and try again.

```
model2.load_weights(checkpoint_path)
loss,acc = model2.evaluate(test_images, test_labels)
print("Second model, accuracy: {:5.2f}%".format(100*acc))
```

We should get this result:

```
5000/5000 [==============================] - 0s 50us/step
Restored model, accuracy: 92.06%
```

That makes again sense, since the new model is now using the weights on the old trained model. Keep in mind that, to load pre-trained weights in a new model, the new model needs to have the exact same architecture as the original one.

Note   To use saved weights with a new model, the new model must have the same architecture as the one used to save the weights. Using pre-trained weights can save you a lot of time, since you don't need to waste time training the network again.

As we will see again and again, the basic idea is to use callbacks and define a custom one that will save our weights. Of course, we can customize our callback function. For example, if want to save the weights every 100 epochs, each time with a different filename so that we can restore a specific checkpoint if needed, we must first define the filename in a dynamic way:

```
checkpoint_path = "training/cp-{epoch:04d}.ckpt"
checkpoint_dir = os.path.dirname(checkpoint_path)
```

We should also use the following callback:

```
cp_callback = tf.keras.callbacks.ModelCheckpoint(
    checkpoint_path, verbose=1, save_weights_only=True,
    period=1)
```

Note that checkpoint_path can contain named formatting options (in the name we have {epoch:04d}), which will be filled by the values of epoch and keys in logs (passed in on_epoch_end, which we saw in the previous

section).[9] You can check the original code for `tf.keras.callbacks.`
`ModelCheckpoint` and you will find that the formatting is done in the `on_`
`epoch_end(self, epoch, logs)` method:

```
filepath = self.filepath.format(epoch=epoch + 1, **logs)
```

You can define your filename with the epoch number and the values
contained in the `logs` dictionary.

Let's get back to our example. Let's start by saving the first version of
the model:

```
model.save_weights(checkpoint_path.format(epoch=0))
```

Then we can fit the model as usual:

```
model.fit(train_images, train_labels,
          epochs = 10, callbacks = [cp_callback],
          validation_data = (test_images,test_labels),
          verbose=0)
```

Be careful since this will save lots of files. In our example, one file
every epoch. So, for example, your directory content (obtainable with `!ls`
`training`) may look like this:

```
checkpoint                         cp-0006.ckpt.data-00000-of-00001
cp-0000.ckpt.data-00000-of-00001   cp-0006.ckpt.index
cp-0000.ckpt.index                 cp-0007.ckpt.data-00000-of-00001
cp-0001.ckpt.data-00000-of-00001   cp-0007.ckpt.index
cp-0001.ckpt.index                 cp-0008.ckpt.data-00000-of-00001
cp-0002.ckpt.data-00000-of-00001   cp-0008.ckpt.index
cp-0002.ckpt.index                 cp-0009.ckpt.data-00000-of-00001
cp-0003.ckpt.data-00000-of-00001   cp-0009.ckpt.index
cp-0003.ckpt.index                 cp-0010.ckpt.data-00000-of-00001
```

---

[9]Check the official documentation at `https://goo.gl/SnKgyQ`.

```
cp-0004.ckpt.data-00000-of-00001  cp-0010.ckpt.index
cp-0004.ckpt.index                cp.ckpt.data-00000-of-00001
cp-0005.ckpt.data-00000-of-00001  cp.ckpt.index
cp-0005.ckpt.index
```

A last tip before moving on is how to get the latest checkpoint, without bothering to search its filename. This can be done easily with the following code:

```
latest = tf.train.latest_checkpoint('training')
model.load_weights(latest)
```

This will load the weights saved in the latest checkpoint automatically. The latest variable is simply a string and contains the last checkpoint filename. In our example, that is training/cp-0010.ckpt.

Note The checkpoint files are binary files that contain the weights of your model. So you will not be able to read them directly, and you should not need to.

Save Your Weights Manually

Of course, you can simply save your model weights manually when you are done training, without defining a callback function:

```
model.save_weights('./checkpoints/my_checkpoint')
```

This command will generate three files, all starting with the string you gave as a name. In this case, it's my_checkpoint. Running the previous code will generate the three files we described above:

```
checkpoint
my_checkpoint.data-00000-of-00001
my_checkpoint.index
```

Reloading the weights in a new model is as simple as this:

```
model.load_weights('./checkpoints/my_checkpoint')
```

Keep in mind that, to be able to reload saved weights in a new model, the old model must have the same architecture as the new one. It must be exactly the same.

Saving the Entire Model

Keras also allows you to save the entire model on disk: weights, the architecture, and the optimizer. In this way, you can recreate the same model by moving some files. For example, we could use the following code

```
model.save('my_model.h5')
```

This will save in one file, called my_model.h5, the entire model. You can simply move the file to a different computer and recreate the same trained model with this code:

```
new_model = keras.models.load_model('my_model.h5')
```

Note that this model will have the same trained weights of your original model, so it's ready to use. This may be helpful if you want to stop training your model and continue the training on a different machine, for example. Or maybe you must stop the training for a while and continue at a later time.

Dataset Abstraction

The tf.data.Dataset[10] is a new abstraction in TensorFlow that is very useful for building data pipelines. It's also very useful when you are dealing with datasets that do not fit in memory. We will see how to use it in more

---

[10]https://www.tensorflow.org/guide/datasets

detail later in the book. In the next sections, I give you some hints on a couple of ways in which you can use it in your projects. To learn how to use it, a good starting point is to study the official documentation at https://www.tensorflow.org/guide/datasets. Remember: Always start there when you want to learn more about a specific method or feature of TensorFlow.

Basically, a Dataset it is simply a sequence of elements, in which each element contains one or more tensors. Typically, each element will be one training example or a batch of them. The basic idea is that first you create a Dataset with some data, and then you chain method calls on it. For example, you apply the Dataset.map() to apply a function to each element. Note that a dataset is made up of elements, each with the same structure.

As usual, let's consider an example to understand how this works and how to use it. Let's suppose we have as input a matrix of 10 rows and 10 columns, defined by the following:

```
inp = tf.random_uniform([10, 10])
```

We can simply create a dataset with the following:

```
dataset = tf.data.Dataset.from_tensor_slices(inp)
```

Using print(dataset), will get you this output:

```
<TensorSliceDataset shapes: (10,), types: tf.float32>
```

That tells you that each element in the dataset is a tensor with 10 elements (the rows in the inp tensor). A nice possibility is to apply specific functions to each element in a dataset. For example, we could multiply all elements by two:

```
dataset2 = dataset.map(lambda x: x*2)
```

In order to check what happened, we could print the first element in each dataset. This can be easily done (more on that later) with:

```
dataset.make_one_shot_iterator().get_next()
```

and

```
dataset2.make_one_shot_iterator().get_next()
```

From the first line, you will get (your number will be different since we are dealing with random numbers here):

```
<tf.Tensor: id=62, shape=(10,), dtype=float32, numpy=
array([0.2215631 , 0.32099664, 0.04410303, 0.8502971 ,
0.2472974 , 0.25522232, 0.94817066, 0.7719344 , 0.60333145,
0.75336015], dtype=float32)>
```

And from the second line, you get:

```
<tf.Tensor: id=71, shape=(10,), dtype=float32, numpy=
array([0.4431262 , 0.6419933 , 0.08820605, 1.7005942 ,
0.4945948 , 0.51044464, 1.8963413 , 1.5438688 , 1.2066629 ,
1.5067203 ], dtype=float32)>
```

As expected, the second output contains all numbers of the first multiplied by two.

Note   `tf.data.dataset` is designed to build data processing pipelines. For example, in image recognition you could do data augmentation, preparation, normalization, and so on in this way.

I strongly suggest you check the official documentation to get more information on different ways of applying a function to each element. For example, you may need to apply transformation to the data and then flatten the result (see flat_map(), for example).

Iterating Over a Dataset

Once you have your dataset, you probably want to process the elements one by one, or in batches. To do that, you need an iterator. For example, to process the elements that you defined before one by one, you can instantiate a so-called make_one_shot_iterator() as follows:

```
iterator = dataset.make_one_shot_iterator()
```

Then you can iterate over the elements using the get_next() method:

```
for i in range(10):
  value = print(iterator.get_next())
```

This will give you all the elements in the dataset. They will look like this one (note that your number will be different):

```
tf.Tensor(
[0.2215631  0.32099664 0.04410303
0.8502971  0.2472974  0.25522232
 0.94817066 0.7719344  0.60333145 0.75336015], shape=(10,),
 dtype=float32)
```

Note that once you reach the end of the dataset, using the method get_next() will raise a tf.errors.OutOfRangeError.

Simple Batching

The most fundamental way to batch consists of stacking n consecutive elements of a dataset in a single group. This will be very useful when we train our networks with mini-batches. This can be done using the batch() method. Let's get back to our example. Remember that our dataset has 10 elements. Suppose we want to create batches, each having two elements. This can be done with this code:

```
batched_dataset = dataset.batch(2)
```

Now let's define an iterator again with:

```
iterator = batched_dataset.make_one_shot_iterator()
```

Now let's check what get_next() will return with this:

```
print(iterator.get_next())
```

The output will be:

```
tf.Tensor(
[[0.2215631  0.32099664 0.04410303
0.8502971  0.2472974  0.25522232
  0.94817066 0.7719344  0.60333145 0.75336015]
 [0.28381765 0.3738917  0.8146689  0.20919728
 0.5753969  0.9356725
  0.7362906  0.76200795 0.01308048 0.14003313]], shape=(2, 10),
  dtype=float32)
```

That is two elements of our dataset.

Note   Batching with the batch() method is really useful when we train a neural network with mini-batches. We don't have to bother creating the batches ourselves, as tf.data.dataset will do it for us.

Simple Batching with the MNIST Dataset

To try the following code, you may want to restart the kernel you are using to avoid to conflicts with eager execution from the previous examples. Once you have done that, load the data (as before):

```
num_classes = 10

mnist = tf.keras.datasets.mnist
(x_train, y_train), (x_test, y_test) = mnist.load_data()

image_vector_size = 28*28
x_train = x_train.reshape(x_train.shape[0], image_vector_size)
x_test = x_test.reshape(x_test.shape[0], image_vector_size)

y_train = keras.utils.to_categorical(y_train, num_classes)
y_test = keras.utils.to_categorical(y_test, num_classes)
```

Then create the training Dataset:

```
mnist_ds_train = tf.data.Dataset.from_tensor_slices((x_train,
y_train))
```

Now build the Keras model using a simple feed-forward network with two layers:

```
img = tf.placeholder(tf.float32, shape=(None, 784))
x = Dense(128, activation='relu')(img)  # fully-connected layer
with 128 units and ReLU activation
x = Dense(128, activation='relu')(x)
preds = Dense(10, activation='softmax')(x)
labels = tf.placeholder(tf.float32, shape=(None, 10))
loss = tf.reduce_mean(categorical_crossentropy(labels, preds))

correct_prediction = tf.equal(tf.argmax(preds,1),
tf.argmax(labels,1))
```

```
accuracy = tf.reduce_mean(tf.cast(correct_prediction,
tf.float32))
```

```
train_step = tf.train.AdamOptimizer(0.001).minimize(loss)
init_op = tf.global_variables_initializer()
```

Now we need to define the batch size:

```
train_batched = mnist_ds_train.batch(1000)
```

And now let's define the iterator:

```
train_iterator = train_batched.make_initializable_iterator()
# So we can restart from the beginning
next_batch = train_iterator.get_next()
it_init_op = train_iterator.initializer
```

The it_init_op operation will be used to reset the iterator and will start from the beginning of each epoch. Note that the next_batch operation has the following structure:

```
(<tf.Tensor 'IteratorGetNext_6:0' shape=(?, 784) dtype=uint8>,
<tf.Tensor 'IteratorGetNext_6:1' shape=(?, 10) dtype=float32>)
```

Since it contains the images and the labels. During our training, we will need to get the batches in this form:

```
train_batch_x, train_batch_y = sess.run(next_batch)
```

Finally, let's train our network:

```
with tf.Session() as sess:
    sess.run(init_op)

    for epoch in range(50):
        sess.run(it_init_op)
        try:
```

```
  while True:
    train_batch_x, train_batch_y = sess.run(next_batch)
    sess.run(train_step,feed_dict={img: train_batch_x,
    labels: train_batch_y})
except tf.errors.OutOfRangeError:
  pass

if (epoch % 10 == 0 ):
  print('epoch',epoch)
  print(sess.run(accuracy,feed_dict={img: x_train,
                          labels: y_train}))
```

Now, I have used a few tricks here that are good to know. In particular, since you don't know how many batches you have, you can use the following construct to avoid getting error messages:

```
try:
  while True:
    # Do something
except tf.errors.OutOfRangeError:
  pass
```

This way, when you get an OutOfRangeError when you run out of batches, the exception will simply go on without interrupting your code. Note how, for each epoch, we call this code to reset the iterator:

```
sess.run(it_init_op)
```

Otherwise, we would get an OutOfRangeError immediately. Running this code will get you to roughly 99% accuracy very fast. You should see output like this one (I show the output for epoch 40 only, for brevity):

```
epoch 40
0.98903334
```

This quick overview of the dataset is not exhaustive by any means, but should give you an idea of its power. If you want to learn more, the best place to do so is, as usual, the official documentation.

Note   `tf.data.Dataset` is an extremely convenient way of building pipelines for data, beginning from loading, to manipulating, normalizing, augmenting, and so on. Especially in image-recognition problems, this can be very useful. Remember that using it means adding nodes to your computational graph. So no data is processed until the session evaluates the graph.

Using tf.data.Dataset in Eager Execution Mode

This chapter ends with one final hint. If you are working in eager execution mode, your life with datasets is even easier. For example, to iterate over a batched dataset, you can simply do as you would do with classical Python (`for x in ...`). To understand what I mean, let's look at an easy example. First, you need to enable eager execution:

```
import tensorflow as tf
from tensorflow import keras
import tensorflow.contrib.eager as tfe

tf.enable_eager_execution()
```

Then you can simply do this:

```
dataset = tf.data.Dataset.from_tensor_slices(tf.random_
uniform([4, 2]))
dataset = dataset.batch(2)
for batch in dataset:
  print(batch)
```

This can be very useful when you need to iterate over a dataset batch by batch. The output would be as follows (your numbers will be different, due to the `tf.random.uniform()` call):

```
tf.Tensor(
[[0.07181489 0.46992648]
 [0.00652897 0.9028846 ]], shape=(2, 2), dtype=float32)
tf.Tensor(
[[0.9167508  0.8379569 ]
 [0.33501422 0.3299384 ]], shape=(2, 2), dtype=float32)
```

Conclusions

This chapter had the goal of showing you a few techniques that we will use in this book and that will be very helpful to your projects. The goal was not to explain those methods in detail, as that would require a separate book. But the chapter should point you in the right direction when trying to do specific things, such as saving the weights of your model regularly. In the next chapters, we will use some of these techniques. If you want to learn a bit more about them, remember to always check the official documentation.

CHAPTER 3

Fundamentals of Convolutional Neural Networks

In this chapter, we will look at the main components of a convolutional neural network (CNN): kernels and pooling layers. We will then look at how a typical network looks. We will then try to solve a classification problem with a simple convolutional network and try to visualize the convolutional operation. The purpose of this is to try to understand, at least intuitively, how the learning works.

Kernels and Filters

One of the main components of CNNs are filters, which are square matrices that have dimensions $n_K \times n_K$, where n_K is an integer and is usually a small number, like 3 or 5. Sometimes filters are also called *kernels*. Using kernels comes from classical image processing techniques. If you have used Photoshop or similar software, you are used to do operations like

© Umberto Michelucci 2019
U. Michelucci, *Advanced Applied Deep Learning*,
https://doi.org/10.1007/978-1-4842-4976-5_3

sharpening, blurring, embossing, and so on.[1] All those operations are done with kernels. We will see in this section what exactly kernels are and how they work. Note that in this book we will use both terms (kernels and filters) interchangeably. Let's define four different filters and let's check later in the chapter their effect when used in convolution operations. For those examples, we will work with 3×3 filters. For the moment, just take the following definitions as a reference and we will see how to use them later in the chapter.

- The following kernel will allow the detection of horizontal edges

$$\mathfrak{I}_H = \begin{pmatrix} 1 & 1 & 1 \\ 0 & 0 & 0 \\ -1 & -1 & -1 \end{pmatrix}$$

- The following kernel will allow the detection of vertical edges

$$\mathfrak{I}_V = \begin{pmatrix} 1 & 0 & -1 \\ 1 & 0 & -1 \\ 1 & 0 & -1 \end{pmatrix}$$

- The following kernel will allow the detection of edges when luminosity changes drastically

$$\mathfrak{I}_L = \begin{pmatrix} -1 & -1 & -1 \\ -1 & 8 & -1 \\ -1 & -1 & -1 \end{pmatrix}$$

---

[1]You can find a nice overview on Wikipedia at `https://en.wikipedia.org/wiki/Kernel_(image_processing)`.

- The following kernel will blur edges in an image

$$\mathfrak{I}_B = -\frac{1}{9} \begin{pmatrix} 1 & 1 & 1 \\ 1 & 1 & 1 \\ 1 & 1 & 1 \end{pmatrix}$$

In the next sections, we will apply convolution to a test image with the filters, to see what their effect is.

Convolution

The first step to understanding CNNs is to understand convolution. The easiest way is to see it in action with a few simple cases. First, in the context of neural networks, convolution is done between tensors. The operation gets two tensors as input and produces a tensor as output. The operation is usually indicated with the operator *.

Let's see how it works. Consider two tensors, both with dimensions 3×3. The convolution operation is done by applying the following formula:

$$\begin{pmatrix} a_1 & a_2 & a_3 \\ a_4 & a_5 & a_6 \\ a_7 & a_8 & a_9 \end{pmatrix} * \begin{pmatrix} k_1 & k_2 & k_3 \\ k_4 & k_5 & k_6 \\ k_7 & k_8 & k_9 \end{pmatrix} = \sum_{i=1}^{9} a_i k_i$$

In this case, the result is merely the sum of each element, a_i, multiplied by the respective element, k_i. In more typical matrix formalism, this formula could be written with a double sum as

$$\begin{pmatrix} a_{11} & a_{12} & a_{13} \\ a_{21} & a_{22} & a_{23} \\ a_{31} & a_{32} & a_{33} \end{pmatrix} * \begin{pmatrix} k_{11} & k_{12} & k_{13} \\ k_{21} & k_{22} & k_{23} \\ k_{31} & k_{32} & k_{33} \end{pmatrix} = \sum_{i=1}^{3} \sum_{j=1}^{3} a_{ij} k_{ij}$$

However, the first version has the advantage of making the fundamental idea very clear: each element from one tensor is multiplied by the correspondent element (the element in the same position) of the second tensor, and then all the values are summed to get the result.

In the previous section, we talked about kernels, and the reason is that convolution is usually done between a tensor, that we may indicate here with A, and a kernel. Typically, kernels are small, 3×3 or 5×5, while the input tensors A are normally bigger. In image recognition for example, the input tensors A are the images that may have dimensions as high as $1024 \times 1024 \times 3$, where 1024×1024 is the resolution and the last dimension (3) is the number of the color channels, the RGB values.

In advanced applications, the images may even have higher resolution. To understand how to apply convolution when we have matrices with different dimensions, let's consider a matrix A that is 4×4

$$
A = \begin{pmatrix} a_1 & a_2 & a_3 & a_4 \\ a_5 & a_6 & a_7 & a_8 \\ a_9 & a_{10} & a_{11} & a_{12} \\ a_{13} & a_{14} & a_{15} & a_{16} \end{pmatrix}
$$

And a Kernel K that we will take for this example to be 3×3

$$
K = \begin{pmatrix} k_1 & k_2 & k_3 \\ k_4 & k_5 & k_6 \\ k_7 & k_8 & k_9 \end{pmatrix}
$$

The idea is to start in the top-left corner of the matrix A and select a 3×3 region. In the example that would be

$$
A_1 = \begin{pmatrix} a_1 & a_2 & a_3 \\ a_5 & a_6 & a_7 \\ a_9 & a_{10} & a_{11} \end{pmatrix}
$$

Alternatively, the elements marked in boldface here:

$$A = \begin{pmatrix} \boldsymbol{a_1} & \boldsymbol{a_2} & \boldsymbol{a_3} & a_4 \\ \boldsymbol{a_5} & \boldsymbol{a_6} & \boldsymbol{a_7} & a_8 \\ \boldsymbol{a_9} & \boldsymbol{a_{10}} & \boldsymbol{a_{11}} & a_{12} \\ a_{13} & a_{14} & a_{15} & a_{16} \end{pmatrix}$$

Then we perform the convolution, as explained at the beginning between this smaller matrix A_1 and K, getting (we will indicate the result with B_1):

$$B_1 = A_1 * K = a_1 k_1 + a_2 k_2 + a_3 k_3 + k_4 a_5 + k_5 a_5 + k_6 a_7 + k_7 a_9 + k_8 a_{10} + k_9 a_{11}$$

Then we need to shift the selected 3×3 region in matrix A of one column to the right and select the elements marked in bold here:

$$A = \begin{pmatrix} a_1 & \boldsymbol{a_2} & \boldsymbol{a_3} & \boldsymbol{a_4} \\ a_5 & \boldsymbol{a_6} & \boldsymbol{a_7} & \boldsymbol{a_8} \\ a_9 & \boldsymbol{a_{10}} & \boldsymbol{a_{11}} & \boldsymbol{a_{12}} \\ a_{13} & a_{14} & a_{15} & a_{16} \end{pmatrix}$$

This will give us the second sub-matrix A_2:

$$A_2 = \begin{pmatrix} a_2 & a_3 & a_4 \\ a_6 & a_7 & a_8 \\ a_{10} & a_{11} & a_{12} \end{pmatrix}$$

We then perform the convolution between this smaller matrix A_2 and K again:

$$B_2 = A_2 * K = a_2 k_1 + a_3 k_2 + a_4 k_3 + a_6 k_4 + a_7 k_5 + a_8 k_6 + a_{10} k_7 + a_{11} k_8 + a_{12} k_9$$

We cannot shift our 3×3 region anymore to the right, since we have reached the end of the matrix A, so what we do is shift it one row down and start again from the left side. The next selected region would be

$$A_3 = \begin{pmatrix} a_5 & a_6 & a_7 \\ a_9 & a_{10} & a_{11} \\ a_{13} & a_{14} & a_{15} \end{pmatrix}$$

Again, we perform convolution of A_3 with K

$$B_3 = A_3 * K = a_5 k_1 + a_6 k_2 + a_7 k_3 + a_9 k_4 + a_{10} k_5 + a_{11} k_6 + a_{13} k_7 + a_{14} k_8 + a_{15} k_9$$

As you may have guessed at this point, the last step is to shift our 3×3 selected region to the right of one column and perform convolution again. Our selected region will now be

$$A_4 = \begin{pmatrix} a_6 & a_7 & a_8 \\ a_{10} & a_{11} & a_{12} \\ a_{14} & a_{15} & a_{16} \end{pmatrix}$$

Moreover, the convolution will give this result:

$$B_4 = A_4 * K = a_6 k_1 + a_7 k_2 + a_8 k_3 + a_{10} k_4 + a_{11} k_5 + a_{12} k_6 + a_{14} k_7 + a_{15} k_8 + a_{16} k_9$$

Now we cannot shift our 3×3 region anymore, neither right nor down. We have calculated four values: B_1, B_2, B_3, and B_4. Those elements will form the resulting tensor of the convolution operation giving us the tensor B:

$$B = \begin{pmatrix} B_1 & B_2 \\ B_3 & B_4 \end{pmatrix}$$

The same process can be applied when tensor A is bigger. You will simply get a bigger resulting B tensor, but the algorithm to get the elements B_i is the same. Before moving on, there is still a small detail that we need to discuss, and that is the concept of stride. In the previous process, we moved our 3×3 region always one column to the right and one row down. The number of rows and columns, in this example 1, is called the *stride* and is often indicated with s. Stride $s = 2$ means simply that we shift our 3×3 region two columns to the right and two rows down at each step.

Something else that we need to discuss is the size of the selected region in the input matrix A. The dimensions of the selected region that we shifted around in the process must be the same as of the kernel used. If you use a 5×5 kernel, you will need to select a 5×5 region in A. In general, given a $n_K \times n_K$ kernel, you select a $n_K \times n_K$ region in A.

In a more formal definition, convolution with stride s in the neural network context is a process that takes a tensor A of dimensions $n_A \times n_A$ and a kernel K of dimensions $n_K \times n_K$ and gives as output a matrix B of dimensions $n_B \times n_B$ with

$$n_B = \left\lfloor \frac{n_A - n_K}{s} + 1 \right\rfloor$$

Where we have indicated with $\lfloor x \rfloor$ the integer part of x (in the programming world, this is often called the floor of x). A proof of this formula would take too long to discuss, but it's easy to see why it is true (try to derive it). To make things a bit easier, suppose that n_K is odd. You will see soon why this is important (although not fundamental). Let's start explaining formally the case with a stride $s = 1$. The algorithm generates a new tensor B from an input tensor A and a kernel K according to the formula

$$B_{ij} = \left(A * K \right)_{ij} = \sum_{f=0}^{n_K-1} \sum_{h=0}^{n_K-1} A_{i+f,j+h} K_{i+f,j+h}$$

The formula is cryptic and is very difficult to understand. Let's study some more examples to grasp the meaning better. In Figure 3-1, you can see a visual explanation of how convolution works. Suppose to have a 3 × 3 filter. Then in the Figure 3-1, you can see that the top left nine elements of the matrix A, marked by a square drawn with a black continuous line, are the one used to generate the first element of the matrix B_1 according to this formula. The elements marked by the square drawn with a dotted line are the ones used to generate the second element B_2 and so on.

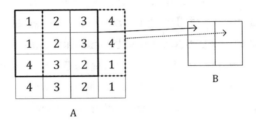

Figure 3-1. *A visual explanation of convolution*

To reiterate what we discuss in the example at the beginning, the basic idea is that each element of the 3 × 3 square from matrix A is multiplied by the corresponding element of the kernel K and all the numbers are summed. The sum is then the element of the new matrix B. After having calculated the value for B_1, you shift the region you are considering in the original matrix of one column to the right (the square indicated in Figure 3-1 with a dotted line) and repeat the operation. You continue to shift your region to the right until you reach the border and then you move one element down and start again from the left. You continue in this fashion until the lower right angle of the matrix. The same kernel is used for all the regions in the original matrix.

Given the kernel $\Im_H$ for example, you can see in Figure 3-2 which element of A are multiplied by which elements in $\Im_H$ and the result for the element B_1, that is nothing else as the sum of all the multiplications

$$B_{11} = 1 \times 1 + 2 \times 1 + 3 \times 1 + 1 \times 0 + 2 \times 0 + 3 \times 0 + 4 \times (-1) + 3 \times (-1) + 2 \times (-1) = -3$$

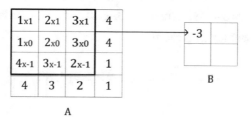

Figure 3-2. *A visualization of convolution with the kernel $\mathfrak{I}_H$*

In Figure 3-3, you can see an example of convolution with stride $s = 2$.

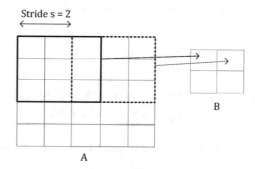

Figure 3-3. *A visual explanation of convolution with stride $s = 2$*

The reason that the dimension of the output matrix takes only the floor (the integer part) of

$$\frac{n_A - n_K}{s} + 1$$

Can be seen intuitively in Figure 3-4. If $s > 1$, what can happen, depending on the dimensions of A, is that at a certain point you cannot shift your window on matrix A (the black square you can see in Figure 3-3 for example) anymore, and you cannot cover all of matrix A completely. In Figure 3-4, you can see how you would need an additional column to the right of matrix A (marked by many X) to be able to perform the convolution operation. In Figure 3-4, we chose $s = 3$, and since we have $n_A = 5$ and $n_K = 3$, B will be a scalar as a result.

$$n_B = \left\lfloor \frac{n_A - n_K}{s} + 1 \right\rfloor = \left\lfloor \frac{5-3}{3} + 1 \right\rfloor = \left\lfloor \frac{5}{3} \right\rfloor = 1$$

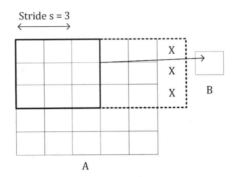

Figure 3-4. *A visual explanation of why the floor function is needed when evaluating the resulting matrix B dimensions*

You can easily see from Figure 3-4, how with a 3 × 3 region, one can only cover the top-left region of A, since with stride $s = 3$ you would end up outside A and therefore can consider one region only for the convolution operation. Therefore, you end up with a scalar for the resulting tensor B.

Let's now look at a few additional examples to make this formula even more transparent. Let's start with a small matrix 3 × 3

$$A = \begin{pmatrix} 1 & 2 & 3 \\ 4 & 5 & 6 \\ 7 & 8 & 9 \end{pmatrix}$$

Moreover, let's consider the kernel

$$K = \begin{pmatrix} k_1 & k_2 & k_3 \\ k_4 & k_5 & k_6 \\ k_7 & k_8 & k_9 \end{pmatrix}$$

with stride $s = 1$. The convolution will be given by

$$B = A * K = 1 \cdot k_1 + 2 \cdot k_2 + 3 \cdot k_3 + 4 \cdot k_4 + 5 \cdot k_5 + 6 \cdot k_6 + 7 \cdot k_7 + 8 \cdot k_8 + 9 \cdot k_9$$

Moreover, the result B will be a scalar, since $n_A = 3$, $n_K = 3$.

$$n_B = \left\lfloor \frac{n_A - n_K}{s} + 1 \right\rfloor = \left\lfloor \frac{3-3}{1} + 1 \right\rfloor = 1$$

If you consider a matrix A with dimensions 4×4, or $n_A = 4$, $n_K = 3$ and $s = 1$, you will get as output a matrix B with dimensions 2×2, since

$$n_B = \left\lfloor \frac{n_A - n_K}{s} + 1 \right\rfloor = \left\lfloor \frac{4-3}{1} + 1 \right\rfloor = 2$$

For example, you can verify that given

$$A = \begin{pmatrix} 1 & 2 & 3 & 4 \\ 5 & 6 & 7 & 8 \\ 9 & 10 & 11 & 12 \\ 13 & 14 & 15 & 16 \end{pmatrix}$$

And

$$K = \begin{pmatrix} 1 & 2 & 3 \\ 4 & 5 & 6 \\ 7 & 8 & 9 \end{pmatrix}$$

We have with stride $s = 1$

$$B = A * K = \begin{pmatrix} 348 & 393 \\ 528 & 573 \end{pmatrix}$$

We'll verify one of the elements: B_{11} with the formula I gave you. We have

$$B_{11} = \sum_{f=0}^{2}\sum_{h=0}^{2} A_{1+f,1+h}K_{1+f,1+h} = \sum_{f=0}^{2}\left(A_{1+f,1}K_{1+f,1} + A_{1+f,2}K_{1+f,2} + A_{1+f,3}K_{1+f,3}\right)$$

$$= \left(A_{1,1}K_{1,1} + A_{1,2}K_{1,2} + A_{1,3}K_{1,3}\right) + \left(A_{2,1}K_{2,1} + A_{2,2}K_{2,2} + A_{2,3}K_{2,3}\right)$$

$$+ \left(A_{3,1}K_{3,1} + A_{3,2}K_{3,2} + A_{3,3}K_{3,3}\right) = (1\cdot1 + 2\cdot2 + 3\cdot3) + (5\cdot4 + 6\cdot5 + 7\cdot6)$$

$$+ (9\cdot7 + 10\cdot8 + 11\cdot9) = 14 + 92 + 242 = 348$$

Note that the formula I gave you for the convolution works only for stride $s = 1$, but can be easily generalized for other values of s.

This calculation is very easy to implement in Python. The following function can evaluate the convolution of two matrices easily enough for $s = 1$ (you can do it in Python with existing functions, but I think it's instructive to see how to do it from scratch):

```python
import numpy as np
def conv_2d(A, kernel):
    output = np.zeros([A.shape[0]-(kernel.shape[0]-1),
    A.shape[1]-(kernel.shape[0]-1)])

    for row in range(1,A.shape[0]-1):
        for column in range(1, A.shape[1]-1):
            output[row-1, column-1] = np.tensordot(A[row-
            1:row+2, column-1:column+2], kernel)

    return output
```

Note that the input matrix A does not even need to a square one, but it is assumed that the kernel is and that its dimension n_K is odd. The previous example can be evaluated with the following code:

```python
A = np.array([[1,2,3,4],[5,6,7,8],[9,10,11,12],[13,14,15,16]])
K = np.array([[1,2,3],[4,5,6],[7,8,9]])
print(conv_2d(A,K))
```

This gives the result:

```
[[ 348. 393.]
 [ 528. 573.]]
```

Examples of Convolution

Now let's try to apply the kernels we defined at the beginning to a test image and see the results. As a test image, let's create a chessboard of dimensions 160×160 pixels with the code:

```
chessboard = np.zeros([8*20, 8*20])
for row in range(0, 8):
    for column in range (0, 8):
        if ((column+8*row) % 2 == 1) and (row % 2 == 0):
            chessboard[row*20:row*20+20,
            column*20:column*20+20] = 1
        elif ((column+8*row) % 2 == 0) and (row % 2 == 1):
            chessboard[row*20:row*20+20,
            column*20:column*20+20] = 1
```

In Figure 3-5, you can see how the chessboard looks.

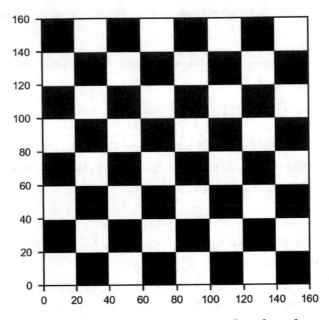

Figure 3-5. *The chessboard image generated with code*

Now let's apply convolution to this image with the different kernels with stride $s = 1$.

Using the kernel, $\mathfrak{J}_H$ will detect the horizontal edges. This can be applied with the code

```
edgeh = np.matrix('1 1 1; 0 0 0; -1 -1 -1')
outputh = conv_2d (chessboard, edgeh)
```

In Figure 3-6, you can see how the output looks. The image can be easily generated with this code:

```
Import matplotlib.pyplot as plt
plt.imshow(outputh)
```

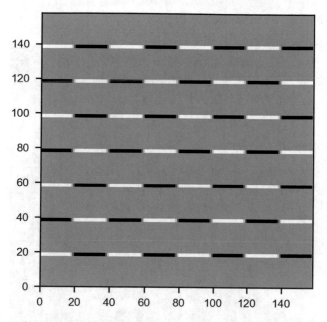

Figure 3-6. *The result of performing a convolution between the kernel* $\mathfrak{I}_H$ *and the chessboard image*

Now you can understand why this kernel detects horizontal edges. Additionally, this kernel detects when you go from light to dark or vice versa. Note this image is only 158 × 158 pixels, as expected, since

$$n_B = \left\lfloor \frac{n_A - n_K}{s} + 1 \right\rfloor = \left\lfloor \frac{160 - 3}{1} + 1 \right\rfloor = \left\lfloor \frac{157}{1} + 1 \right\rfloor = \lfloor 158 \rfloor = 158$$

Now let's apply $\mathfrak{I}_V$ using this code:

```
edgev = np.matrix('1 0 -1; 1 0 -1; 1 0 -1')
outputv = conv_2d (chessboard, edgev)
```

This gives the result shown in Figure 3-7.

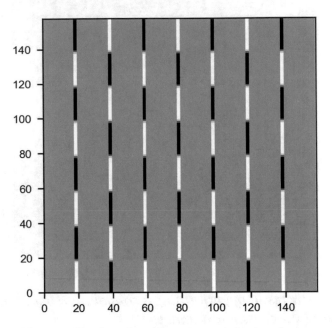

Figure 3-7. *The result of performing a convolution between the kernel $\Im_V$ and the chessboard image*

Now we can use kernel $\Im_L$:

```
edgel = np.matrix ('-1 -1 -1; -1 8 -1; -1 -1 -1')
outputl = conv_2d (chessboard, edgel)
```

That gives the result shown in Figure 3-8.

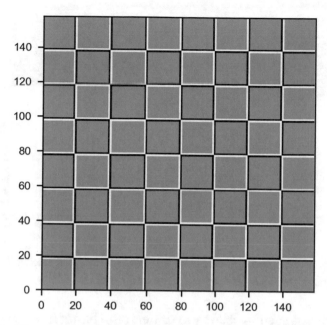

Figure 3-8. *The result of performing a convolution between the kernel* $\mathfrak{I}_L$ *and the chessboard image*

Moreover, we can apply the blurring kernel $\mathfrak{I}_B$:

```
edge_blur = -1.0/9.0*np.matrix('1 1 1; 1 1 1; 1 1 1')
output_blur = conv_2d (chessboard, edge_blur)
```

In Figure 3-9, you can see two plots—on the left the blurred image and on the right the original one. The images show only a small region of the original chessboard to make the blurring clearer.

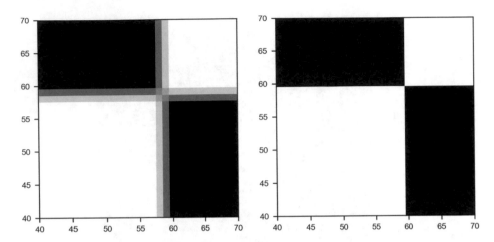

Figure 3-9. *The effect of the blurring kernel* $\mathfrak{I}_B$. *On the left is the blurred image and on the right is the original one.*

To finish this section, let's try to understand better how the edges can be detected. Consider the following matrix with a sharp vertical transition, since the left part is full of 10 and the right part full of 0.

ex_mat = np.matrix('10 10 10 10 0 0 0 0; 10 10 10 10 0 0 0 0; 10 10 10 10 0 0 0 0; 10 10 10 10 0 0 0 0; 10 10 10 10 0 0 0 0; 10 10 10 10 0 0 0 0; 10 10 10 10 0 0 0 0; 10 10 10 10 0 0 0 0')

This looks like this

```
matrix([[10, 10, 10, 10, 0, 0, 0, 0],
        [10, 10, 10, 10, 0, 0, 0, 0],
        [10, 10, 10, 10, 0, 0, 0, 0],
        [10, 10, 10, 10, 0, 0, 0, 0],
        [10, 10, 10, 10, 0, 0, 0, 0],
        [10, 10, 10, 10, 0, 0, 0, 0],
        [10, 10, 10, 10, 0, 0, 0, 0],
        [10, 10, 10, 10, 0, 0, 0, 0]])
```

Let's consider the kernel $\mathfrak{I}_V$. We can perform the convolution with this code:

```
ex_out = conv_2d (ex_mat, edgev)
```

The result is as follows:

```
array([[ 0.,  0., 30., 30.,  0.,  0.],
       [ 0.,  0., 30., 30.,  0.,  0.],
       [ 0.,  0., 30., 30.,  0.,  0.],
       [ 0.,  0., 30., 30.,  0.,  0.],
       [ 0.,  0., 30., 30.,  0.,  0.],
       [ 0.,  0., 30., 30.,  0.,  0.]])
```

In Figure 3-10, you can see the original matrix (on the left) and the output of the convolution on the right. The convolution with the kernel $\mathfrak{I}_V$ has clearly detected the sharp transition in the original matrix, marking with a vertical black line where the transition from black to white happens. For example, consider $B_{11} = 0$

$$B_{11} = \begin{pmatrix} 10 & 10 & 10 \\ 10 & 10 & 10 \\ 10 & 10 & 10 \end{pmatrix} * \mathfrak{I}_V = \begin{pmatrix} 10 & 10 & 10 \\ 10 & 10 & 10 \\ 10 & 10 & 10 \end{pmatrix} * \begin{pmatrix} 1 & 0 & -1 \\ 1 & 0 & -1 \\ 1 & 0 & -1 \end{pmatrix}$$

$$= 10 \times 1 + 10 \times 0 + 10 \times -1 + 10 \times 1 + 10 \times 0 + 10 \times -1 + 10 \times 1 + 10 \times 0 + 10 \times -1 = 0$$

Note that in the input matrix

$$\begin{pmatrix} 10 & 10 & 10 \\ 10 & 10 & 10 \\ 10 & 10 & 10 \end{pmatrix}$$

there is no transition, as all the values are the same. On the contrary, if you consider B_{13} you need to consider this region of the input matrix

$$\begin{pmatrix} 10 & 10 & 0 \\ 10 & 10 & 0 \\ 10 & 10 & 0 \end{pmatrix}$$

where there is a clear transition since the right-most column is made of zeros and the rest of 10. You get now a different result

$$B_{11} = \begin{pmatrix} 10 & 10 & 0 \\ 10 & 10 & 0 \\ 10 & 10 & 0 \end{pmatrix} * \Im_V = \begin{pmatrix} 10 & 10 & 0 \\ 10 & 10 & 0 \\ 10 & 10 & 0 \end{pmatrix} * \begin{pmatrix} 1 & 0 & -1 \\ 1 & 0 & -1 \\ 1 & 0 & -1 \end{pmatrix}$$

$$= 10 \times 1 + 10 \times 0 + 0 \times -1 + 10 \times 1 + 10 \times 0 + 0 \times -1 + 10 \times 1 + 10 \times 0 + 0 \times -1 = 30$$

Moreover, this is precisely how, as soon as there is a significant change in values along the horizontal direction, the convolution returns a high value since the values multiplied by the column with 1 in the kernel will be more significant. When there is a transition from small to high values along the horizontal axis, the elements multiplied by -1 will give a result that is bigger in absolute value. Therefore the final result will be negative and big in absolute value. This is the reason that this kernel can also detect if you pass from a light color to a darker color and vice versa. If you consider the opposite transition (from 0 to 10) in a different hypothetical matrix A, you would have

$$B_{11} = \begin{pmatrix} 0 & 10 & 10 \\ 0 & 10 & 10 \\ 0 & 10 & 10 \end{pmatrix} * \Im_V = \begin{pmatrix} 0 & 10 & 10 \\ 0 & 10 & 10 \\ 0 & 10 & 10 \end{pmatrix} * \begin{pmatrix} 1 & 0 & -1 \\ 1 & 0 & -1 \\ 1 & 0 & -1 \end{pmatrix}$$

$$= 0 \times 1 + 10 \times 0 + 10 \times -1 + 0 \times 1 + 10 \times 0 + 10 \times -1 + 0 \times 1 + 10 \times 0 + 10 \times -1 = -30$$

We move from 0 to 10 along the horizontal direction.

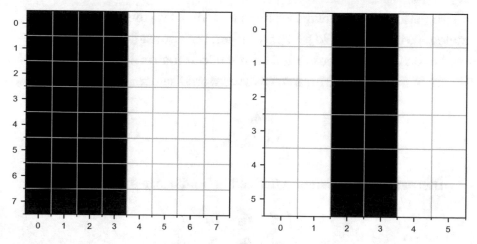

Figure 3-10. *The result of the convolution of the matrix* ex_mat *with the kernel* $\mathfrak{J}_V$ *as described in the text*

Note how, as expected, the output matrix has dimensions 5×5 since the original matrix has dimensions 7×7 and the kernel is 3×3.

Pooling

Pooling is the second operation that is fundamental in CNNs. This operation is much easier to understand than convolution. To understand it, let's look at a concrete example and consider what is called *max pooling*. Consider the 4×4 matrix we discussed during our convolution discussion again:

$$A = \begin{pmatrix} a_1 & a_2 & a_3 & a_4 \\ a_5 & a_6 & a_7 & a_8 \\ a_9 & a_{10} & a_{11} & a_{12} \\ a_{13} & a_{14} & a_{15} & a_{16} \end{pmatrix}$$

To perform max pooling, we need to define a region of size $n_K \times n_K$, analogous to what we did for convolution. Let's consider $n_K = 2$. What we need to do is start on the top-left corner of our matrix A and select a $n_K \times n_K$ region, in our case 2×2 from A. Here we would select

$$\begin{pmatrix} a_1 & a_2 \\ a_5 & a_6 \end{pmatrix}$$

Alternatively, the elements marked in boldface in the matrix A here:

$$A = \begin{pmatrix} \mathbf{a_1} & \mathbf{a_2} & a_3 & a_4 \\ \mathbf{a_5} & \mathbf{a_6} & a_7 & a_8 \\ a_9 & a_{10} & a_{11} & a_{12} \\ a_{13} & a_{14} & a_{15} & a_{16} \end{pmatrix}$$

From the elements selected, a_1, a_2, a_5 and a_6, the max pooling operation selects the maximum value. The result is indicated with B_1

$$B_1 = \max_{i=1,2,5,6} a_i$$

We then need to shift our 2×2 window two columns to the right, typically the same number of columns the selected region has, and select the elements marked in bold:

$$A = \begin{pmatrix} a_1 & a_2 & \mathbf{a_3} & \mathbf{a_4} \\ a_5 & a_6 & \mathbf{a_7} & \mathbf{a_8} \\ a_9 & a_{10} & a_{11} & a_{12} \\ a_{13} & a_{14} & a_{15} & a_{16} \end{pmatrix}$$

Or, in other words, the smaller matrix

$$\begin{pmatrix} a_3 & a_4 \\ a_7 & a_8 \end{pmatrix}$$

The max-pooling algorithm will then select the maximum of the values and give a result that we will indicate with B_2

$$B_2 = \max_{i=3,4,7,8} a_i$$

At this point we cannot shift the 2×2 region to the right anymore, so we shift it two rows down and start the process again from the left side of A, selecting the elements marked in bold and getting the maximum and calling it B_3.

$$A = \begin{pmatrix} a_1 & a_2 & a_3 & a_4 \\ a_5 & a_6 & a_7 & a_8 \\ \mathbf{a_9} & \mathbf{a_{10}} & a_{11} & a_{12} \\ \mathbf{a_{13}} & \mathbf{a_{14}} & a_{15} & a_{16} \end{pmatrix}$$

The stride s in this context has the same meaning we have already discussed in convolution. It's simply the number of rows or columns you move your region when selecting the elements. Finally, we select the last region 2×2 in the bottom-lower part of A, selecting the elements a_{11}, a_{12}, a_{15}, and a_{16}. We then get the maximum and call it B_4. With the values we obtain in this process, in the example the four values B_1, B_2, B_3 and B_4, we will build an output tensor:

$$B = \begin{pmatrix} B_1 & B_2 \\ B_3 & B_4 \end{pmatrix}$$

In the example, we have $s = 2$. Basically, this operation takes as input a matrix A, a stride s, and a kernel size n_K (the dimension of the region we selected in the example before) and returns a new matrix B with dimensions given by the same formula we discussed for convolution:

$$n_B = \left\lfloor \frac{n_A - n_K}{s} + 1 \right\rfloor$$

To reiterate this idea, start from the top-left of matrix A, take a region of dimensions $n_K \times n_K$, apply the max function to the selected elements, then shift the region of s elements toward the right, select a new region again of dimensions $n_K \times n_K$, apply the function to its values, and so on. In Figure 3-11 you can see how you would select the elements from matrix A with stride $s = 2$.

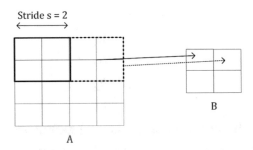

Figure 3-11. *A visualization of pooling with stride $s = 2$*

For example, applying max-pooling to the input A

$$A = \begin{pmatrix} 1 & 3 & 5 & 7 \\ 4 & 5 & 11 & 3 \\ 4 & 1 & 21 & 6 \\ 13 & 15 & 1 & 2 \end{pmatrix}$$

Will get you this result (it's very easy to verify it):

$$B = \begin{pmatrix} 4 & 11 \\ 15 & 21 \end{pmatrix}$$

Since four is the maximum of the values marked in bold.

$$A = \begin{pmatrix} \mathbf{1} & \mathbf{3} & 5 & 7 \\ \mathbf{4} & \mathbf{5} & 11 & 3 \\ 4 & 1 & 21 & 6 \\ 13 & 15 & 1 & 2 \end{pmatrix}$$

Eleven is the maximum of the values marked in bold here:

$$A = \begin{pmatrix} 1 & 3 & \mathbf{5} & \mathbf{7} \\ 4 & 5 & \mathbf{11} & \mathbf{3} \\ 4 & 1 & 21 & 6 \\ 13 & 15 & 1 & 2 \end{pmatrix}$$

And so on. It's worth mentioning another way of doing pooling, although it's not as widely used as max-pooling: ***average pooling***. Instead of returning the maximum of the selected values, it returns the average.

Note   The most commonly used pooling operation is *max pooling*. Average pooling is not as widely used but can be found in specific network architectures.

Padding

Something that's worth mentioning here is *padding*. Sometimes, when dealing with images, it is not optimal to get a result from a convolution operation that has dimensions that are different from the original image. This is when padding is necessary. The idea is straightforward: you add rows of pixels on the top and bottom and columns of pixels on the right and left of the final images so the resulting matrices are the same size as the original. Some strategies fill the added pixels with zeros, with the values of the closest pixels and so on. For example, in our example, our ex_out matrix with zero padding would like like this

```
array([[ 0., 0., 0., 0., 0., 0., 0., 0.],
       [ 0., 0., 0., 30., 30., 0., 0., 0.],
       [ 0., 0., 0., 30., 30., 0., 0., 0.],
       [ 0., 0., 0., 30., 30., 0., 0., 0.],
       [ 0., 0., 0., 30., 30., 0., 0., 0.],
       [ 0., 0., 0., 30., 30., 0., 0., 0.],
       [ 0., 0., 0., 30., 30., 0., 0., 0.],
       [ 0., 0., 0., 0., 0., 0., 0., 0.]])
```

Only as a reference, in case you use padding p (the width of the rows and columns you use as padding), the final dimensions of the matrix B, in case of both convolution and pooling, is given by

$$n_B = \left\lfloor \frac{n_A + 2p - n_K}{s} + 1 \right\rfloor$$

Note   When dealing with real images, you always have color images, coded in three channels: RGB. That means that convolution and pooling must be done in three dimensions: width, height, and color channel. This will add a layer of complexity to the algorithms.

Building Blocks of a CNN

Convolution and pooling operations are used to build the layers used in CNNs. In CNNs typically you can find the following layers

- Convolutional layers

- Pooling layers

- Fully connected layers

Fully connected layers are precisely what we have seen in all the previous chapters: a layer where neurons are connected to all neurons of previous and subsequent layers. You know them already. The other two require some additional explanation.

Convolutional Layers

A convolutional layer takes as input a tensor (which can be three-dimensional, due to the three color channels), for example an image, applies a certain number of kernels, typically 10, 16, or even more, adds a bias, applies ReLu activation functions (for example) to introduce non-linearity to the result of the convolution, and produces an output matrix B.

Now in the previous sections, I showed you some examples of applying convolutions with just one kernel. How can you apply several kernels at the same time? Well, the answer is straightforward. The final tensor (I use now the word tensor since it will not be a simple matrix anymore) B will have not two dimensions but three. Let's indicate the number of kernels you want to apply with n_c (the c is used since sometimes people talk about channels). You simply apply each filter to the input independently and stack the results. So instead of a single matrix B with dimensions $n_B \times n_B$ you get a final tensor $\tilde{B}$ of dimensions $n_B \times n_B \times n_c$. That means that this

$$\tilde{B}_{i,j,1} \quad \forall i,j \in \left[1,n_B\right]$$

Will be the output of convolution of the input image with the first kernel, and

$$\tilde{B}_{i,j,2} \quad \forall i,j \in \left[1,n_B\right]$$

Will be the output of convolution with the second kernel, and so on. The convolution layer simply transforms the input into an output tensor. However, what are the weights in this layer? The weights, or the parameters that the network learns during the training phase, are the elements of the kernel themselves. We discussed that we have n_c kernels, each of $n_K \times n_K$ dimensions. That means that we have $n_K^2 n_c$ parameter in a convolutional layer.

Note The number of parameters that you have in a convolutional layer, $n_K^2 n_c$, is independent from the input image size. This fact helps in reducing overfitting, especially when dealing with large input images.

Sometimes this layer is indicated with the word POOL and then a number. In our case, we could indicate this layer with POOL1. In Figure 3-12, you can see a representation of a convolutional layer. The input image is transformed by applying convolution with n_c kernels in a tensor of dimensions $n_A \times n_A \times n_c$.

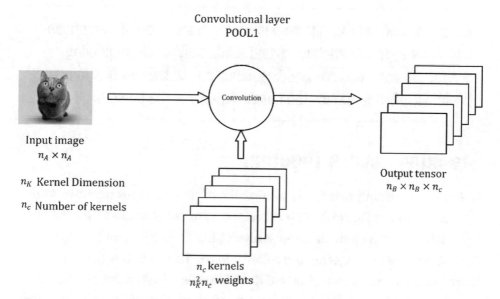

Figure 3-12. *A representation of a convolutional layer[2]*

Of course, a convolutional layer must not necessarily be placed immediately after the inputs. A convolutional layer may get as input the output of any other layer of course. Keep in mind that usually, the input image will have dimensions $n_A \times n_A \times 3$, since an image in color has three channels: Red, Green, and Blue. A complete analysis of the tensors involved in a CNN when considering color images is beyond the scope of this book. Very often in diagrams, the layer is simply indicated as a cube or a square.

---

[2]Cat image source: https://www.shutterstock.com/

Pooling Layers

A pooling layer is usually indicated with POOL and a number: for example, POOL1. It takes as input a tensor and gives as output another tensor after applying pooling to the input.

Note   A pooling layer has no parameter to learn, but it introduces additional hyperparameters: n_K and stride v. Typically, in pooling layers, you don't use any padding, since one of the reasons to use pooling is often to reduce the dimensionality of the tensors.

Stacking Layers Together

In CNNs you usually stack convolutional and pooling layer together. One after the other. In Figure 3-13, you can see a convolutional and a pooling layer stack. A convolutional layer is always followed by a pooling layer. Sometimes the two together are called a *layer*. The reason is that a pooling layer has no learnable weights and therefore it is merely seen as a simple operation that is associated with the convolutional layer. So be aware when you read papers or blogs and check what they intend.

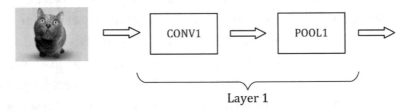

Figure 3-13. *A representation of how to stack convolutional and pooling layers*

To conclude this part of CNN in Figure 3-14, you can see an example of a CNN. In Figure 3-14, you see an example like the very famous LeNet-5 network, about which you can read more here: `https://goo.gl/hM1kAL`. You have the inputs, then two times convolution-pooling layer, then three fully connected layers, and then an output layers, with a `softmax` activation function to perform multiclass classification. I put some indicative numbers in the figure to give you an idea of the size of the different layers.

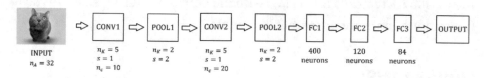

Figure 3-14. *A representation of a CNN similar to the famous LeNet-5 network*

Number of Weights in a CNN

It is important to point out where the weights in a CNN are in the different layers.

Convolutional Layer

In a convolutional layer, the parameters that are learned are the filters themselves. For example, if you have 32 filters, each of dimension 5x5, you will get 32x5x5=832 learnable parameters, since for each filter there is also a bias term that you will need to add. Note that this number is not dependent on the input image size. In a typical feed-forward neural network, the number of weights in the first layer is dependent on the input size, but not here.

CHAPTER 3   FUNDAMENTALS OF CONVOLUTIONAL NEURAL NETWORKS

The number of weights in a convolutional layer is, in general terms, given by the following:

$$n_C \cdot n_K \cdot n_K + n_C$$

Pooling Layer

The pooling layer has no learnable parameters, and as mentioned, this is the reason it's typically associated with the convolutional layer. In this layer (operation), there are no learnable weights.

Dense Layer

In this layer, the weights are the ones you know from traditional feed-forward networks. So the number depends on the number of neurons and the number of neurons in the preceding and subsequent layers.

Note   The only layers in a CNN that have learnable parameters are the convolutional and dense layers.

Example of a CNN: MNIST Dataset

Let's start with some coding. We will develop a very simple CNN and try to do classification on the MNIST dataset. You should know the dataset very well by now, from Chapter 2.

We start, as usual, by importing the necessary packages:

```
from keras.datasets import mnist
from keras.models import Sequential
from keras.layers import Dense, Dropout, Flatten, Conv2D,
MaxPool2D
from keras.utils import np_utils
```

```
import numpy as np
import matplotlib.pyplot as plt
```

We need an additional step before we can start loading the data:

```
from keras import backend as K
K.set_image_dim_ordering('th')
```

The reason is the following. When you load images for your model, you will need to convert them to tensors, each with three dimensions:

- Number of pixels along the x-axis

- Number of pixels along the y-axis

- Number of color channels (in a gray image, this number is; if you have color images, this number is 3, one for each of the RGB channels)

When doing convolution, Keras must know on which axis it finds the information. In particular, it is relevant to define if the index of the color channel's dimension is the first or the last. To achieve this, we can define the ordering of the data with keras.backend.set_image_dim_ordering(). This function accepts as input a string that can assume two possible values:

- 'th' (for the convention used by the library Theano): Theano expects the channel dimensions to be the second one (the first one will be the observation index).

- 'tf' (for the convention used by TensorFlow): TensorFlow expects the channel dimension to be the last one.

You can use both, but simply pay attention when preparing the data to use the right convention. Otherwise, you will get error messages about tensor dimensions. In what follows, we will convert images in tensors having the color channel dimensions as the second one, as you can see later.

Now we are ready to load the MNIST data with this code:

```
(X_train, y_train), (X_test, y_test) = mnist.load_data()
```

The code will deliver the images "flattened," meaning each image will be a one-dimensional vector of 784 elements (28x28). We need to reshape them as proper images, since our convolutional layers want images as inputs. After that, we need to normalize the data (remember the images are in a grayscale, and each pixel can have a value from 0 to 255).

```
X_train = X_train.reshape(X_train.shape[0], 1, 28, 28).
astype('float32')
X_test = X_test.reshape(X_test.shape[0], 1, 28, 28).
astype('float32')
X_train = X_train / 255.0
X_test = X_test / 255.0
```

Note how, since we have defined the ordering as 'th', the number of channels (in this case 1) is the second element of the X arrays. As a next step, we need to one-hot-encode the labels:

```
y_train = np_utils.to_categorical(y_train)
y_test = np_utils.to_categorical(y_test)
```

We know we have 10 classes so we can simply define them:

```
num_classes = 10
```

Now let's define a function to create and compile our Keras model:

```
def baseline_model():
    # create model
    model = Sequential()
    model.add(Conv2D(32, (5, 5), input_shape=(1, 28, 28),
    activation='relu'))
    model.add(MaxPool2D(pool_size=(2, 2)))
```

```
model.add(Dropout(0.2))
model.add(Flatten())
model.add(Dense(128, activation='relu'))
model.add(Dense(num_classes, activation='softmax'))
# Compile model
model.compile(loss='categorical_crossentropy',
optimizer='adam', metrics=['accuracy'])
return model
```

You can see a diagram of this CNN in Figure 3-15.

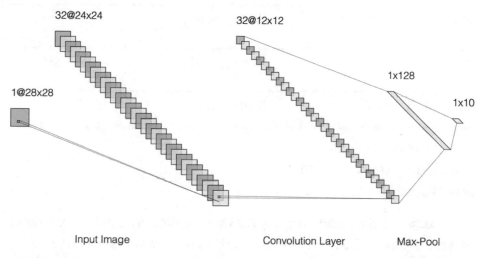

Figure 3-15. *A diagram depicting the CNN we used in the text. The numbers are the dimensions of the tensors produced by each layer.*

To determine what kind of model we have, we simply use the model.summary() call. Let's first create a model and then check it:

```
model = baseline_model()
model.summary()
```

The output (check the diagram form in Figure 3-15) is as follows:

Layer (type)	Output Shape	Param #
conv2d_1 (Conv2D)	(None, 32, 24, 24)	832
max_pooling2d_1 (MaxPooling2	(None, 32, 12, 12)	0
dropout_1 (Dropout)	(None, 32, 12, 12)	0
flatten_1 (Flatten)	(None, 4608)	0
dense_1 (Dense)	(None, 128)	589952
dense_2 (Dense)	(None, 10)	1290

```
Total params: 592,074
Trainable params: 592,074
Non-trainable params: 0
```

In case you are wondering why the max-pooling layer produces tensors of dimensions 12x12, the reason is that since we haven't specified the stride, Keras will take as a standard value the dimension of the filter, which in our case is 2x2. Having input tensors that are 24x24 with stride 2 you will get tensors that are 12x12.

This network is quite simple. In the model we defined just one convolutional and pooling layer, we added a bit of dropout, then we added a dense layer with 128 neurons and then an output layer for the softmax with 10 neurons. Now we can simply train it with the fit() method:

```
model.fit(X_train, y_train, validation_data=(X_test, y_test),
epochs=1, batch_size=200, verbose=1)
```

This will train the network for only one epoch and should give you output similar to this (your numbers may vary a bit):

```
Train on 60000 samples, validate on 10000 samples
Epoch 1/1
60000/60000 [==============================] - 151s 3ms/step -
loss: 0.0735 - acc: 0.9779 - val_loss: 0.0454 - val_acc: 0.9853
```

We have already reached good accuracy, without having any overfitting.

Note   When you pass to the `compile()` method the optimizer parameter, Keras will use its standard parameters. If you want to change them, you need to define an optimizer separately. For example, to specify an Adam optimizer with a starting learning rate of 0.001 you can use `AdamOpt = adam(lr=0.001)` and then pass it to the compile method with `model.compile(optimizer=AdamOpt, loss='categorical_crossentropy', metrics=['accuracy'])`.

Visualization of CNN Learning

Brief Digression: keras.backend.function()

Sometime it's useful to get intermediate results from a computational graph. For example, you may be interested in the output of a specific layer for debugging purposes. In low-level TensorFlow, you can simply evaluate in the session the relevant node in the graph, but it's not so easy to understand how to do it in Keras. To find out, we need to consider what the Keras backend is. The best way of explaining it is to cite the official documentation (`https://keras.io/backend/`):

> *Keras is a model-level library, providing high-level building blocks for developing deep learning models. It does not handle low-level operations such as tensor products, convolutions, and so on itself. Instead, it relies on a specialized, well optimized tensor manipulation library to do so, serving as the "backend engine" of Keras.*

To be complete, it is important to note that Keras uses (at the time of writing) three backends: the *TensorFlow* backend, the *Theano* backend, and the *CNTK* backend. When you want to write your own specific function, you should use the abstract Keras backend API that can be loaded with this code:

```
from keras import backend as K
```

Understanding how to use the Keras backend goes beyond the scope of this book (remember the focus of this book is not Keras), but I suggest you spend some time getting to know it. It may be very useful. For example, to reset a session when using Keras you can use this:

```
keras.backend.clear_session()
```

What we are really interested in this chapter is a specific method available in the backed: `function()`. Its arguments are as follows:

- inputs: List of placeholder tensors

- outputs: List of output tensors

- updates: List of update ops

- `**kwargs`: Passed to `tf.Session.run`

We will use only the first two in this chapter. To understand how to use them, let's consider for example the model we created in the previous sections:

```
model = Sequential()
model.add(Conv2D(32, (5, 5), input_shape=(1, 28, 28),
activation='relu'))
model.add(MaxPool2D(pool_size=(2, 2)))
model.add(Dropout(0.2))
model.add(Flatten())
model.add(Dense(128, activation='relu'))
model.add(Dense(num_classes, activation='softmax'))
```

How do we get, for example, the output of the first convolutional layer? We can do this easily by creating a function:

```
get_1st_layer_output = K.function([model.layers[0].
input],[model.layers[0].output])
```

This will use the following arguments

- inputs: `model.layers[0].input`, which is the input of our network

- outputs: `model.layers[0].output`, which is the output of the first layer (with index 0)

You simply ask Keras to evaluate specific nodes in your computational graph, given a specific set of inputs. Note that up to now we have only defined a function. Now we need to apply it to a specific dataset. For example, if we want to apply it to one single image, we could do this:

```
layer_conv_output = get_1st_layer_output([np.expand_dims(X_
test[21], axis=0)])[0]
```

This multidimensional array will have dimensions $(1, 32, 24, 24)$ as expected: one image, 32 filters, 24x24 output. In the next section, we will use this function to see the effect of the learned filter in the network.

Effect of Kernels

It is interesting to see what the effect of the learned kernels is on the input image. For this purpose, let's take an image from the test dataset (if you shuffled your dataset, you may get a different digit at index 21).

```
tst = X_test[21]
```

Note how this array has dimensions $(1,28,28)$. This is a six, as you can see in Figure 3-16.

Figure 3-16. *The first image in the test dataset*

To get the effect of the first layer (the convolutional one), we can use the following code (explained in the previous section)

```
get_1st_layer_output = K.function([model.layers[0].
input],[model.layers[0].output])
layer_conv_output = get_1st_layer_output([tst])[0]
```

Note how the layer_conv_output is a multidimensional array, and it will contain the convolution of the input image with each filter, stacked on top of each other. Its dimensions are (1,32,24,24). The first number is 1 since we applied the layer only to one single image, the second, 32, is the number of filters we have, and the second is 24 since, as we have discussed, the output tensor dimensions of a conv layer are given by

$$n_B = \left\lfloor \frac{n_A + 2p - n_K}{s} + 1 \right\rfloor$$

Moreover, in our case

$$n_B = \left\lfloor \frac{28 - 5}{1} + 1 \right\rfloor = 24$$

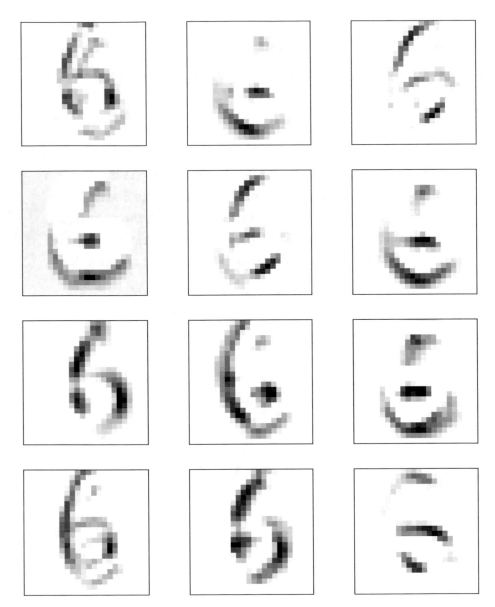

Figure 3-17. *The test image (a 6) convoluted with the first 12 filters learned by the network*

Since in our network, we have $n_A = 28$, $p = 0$, $n_K = 5$, and stride $s = 1$. In Figure 3-17, you can see our test image convoluted with the first 12 filters (32 was too many for a figure).

From Figure 3-17 you can see how different filters learn to detect different features. For example, the third filter (as can be seen in Figure 3-18) learned to detect diagonal lines.

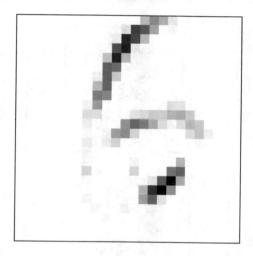

Figure 3-18. *The test image convoluted with the third filter. It learned to detect diagonal lines.*

Other filters learn to detect horizontal lines or other features.

Effect of Max-Pooling

The subsequent step is to apply max pooling to the output of the convolutional layer. As we discussed, this will reduce the dimensions of the tensors and will try to (intuitively) condense the relevant information.

You can see the output on the tensor coming from the first 12 filters in Figure 3-19.

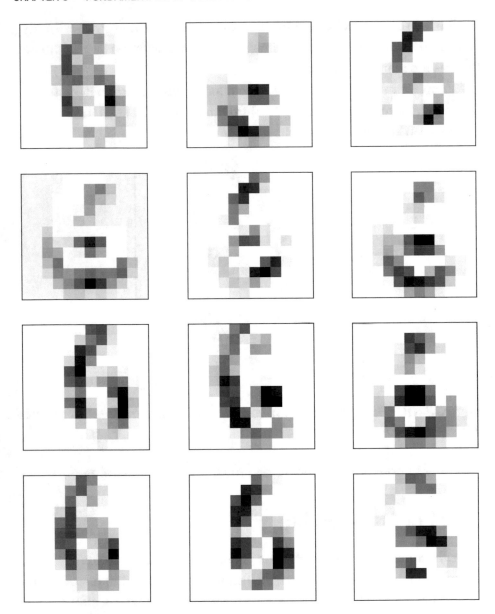

Figure 3-19. *The output of the pooling layer when applied to the first 12 tensors coming from the convolutional layer*

Let's see how our test image is transformed from one convolutional and the pooling layer by one of the filters (consider the third, just for illustration purposes). You can easily see the effect in Figure 3-20.

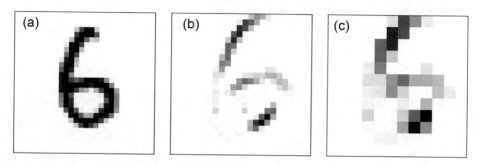

Figure 3-20. *The original test image as in the dataset (in panel a); the image convoluted with the third learned filter (panel b); the image convoluted with the third filter after the max pooling layer (panel c)*

Note how the resolution of the image is changing, since we are not using any padding. In the next chapter, we will look at more complicated architectures, called *inception networks,* that are known to work better than traditional CNN (what we have described in this chapter) when dealing with images. In fact, simply adding more and more convolutional layers will not easily increase the accuracy of the predictions, and more complex architecture are known to be much more effective.

Now that we have seen the very basic building blocks of a CNN, we are ready to move to some more advanced topics. In the next chapter, we will look at many exciting topics as inception networks, multiple loss functions, custom loss functions, and transfer learning.

CHAPTER 4

Advanced CNNs and Transfer Learning

In this chapter, we look at more advanced techniques typically used when developing CNNs. In particular, we will look at a very successful new convolutional network called the *inception network* that is based on the idea of several convolutional operations done in parallel instead of sequentially. We will then look at how to use the multiple cost function, in a similar fashion as what is done in multi-task learning. The next sections will show you how to use the pre-trained network that Keras makes available, and how to use transfer learning to tune those pre-trained networks for your specific problem. At the end of the chapter, we will look at a technique to implement transfer learning that is very efficient when dealing with big datasets.

Convolution with Multiple Channels

In the previous chapter, you learned how convolution works. In the examples we have explicitly described how to perform it when the input is a bi-dimensional matrix. But this is not what happens in reality. For example, the input tensors may represent color images, and therefore will have three dimensions: the number of pixels in the x direction (resolution along the x axis), the number of pixels in the y direction (resolution along

© Umberto Michelucci 2019
U. Michelucci, *Advanced Applied Deep Learning*,
https://doi.org/10.1007/978-1-4842-4976-5_4

the y axis), and the number of color channels, that is three when dealing with RGB images (one channel for the reds, one for the greens, and one for the blues). It can be even worse. A convolutional layer with 32 kernels, each 5×5, when expecting an input of images each 28×28 (see the MNIST example in the previous chapter) will have an output of dimensions $(m, 32, 24, 24)$, where m is the number of training images. That means that our convolutions will have to be done with tensors with dimensions of $32 \times 24 \times 24$. So how we can perform the convolutional operation on three-dimensional tensors? Well, it is actually quite easy. Mathematically speaking, if kernel K has dimensions $n_K \times n_K \times n_c$, and the input tensors A have dimensions $n_x \times n_y \times n_c$, the result of our convolution operation will be:

$$\sum_{i=1}^{n_x} \sum_{j=1}^{n_y} \sum_{k=1}^{n_c} K_{ijk} A_{ijk}$$

Meaning that we will sum over the channel dimension. In Keras, when you define a convolutional layer in 2D, you use the following code:

```
Conv2D(32, (5, 5), input_shape=(1, 28, 28), activation='relu')
```

Where the first number (32) is the number of filters and (5,5) defines the dimensions of the kernels. What Keras does not tell you is that it automatically takes kernels of $n_c \times 5 \times 5$ where n_c is the number of channels of the input tensors. This is why you need to give the first layer the input_ shape parameter. The number of channels is included in this information. But which of the three numbers is the correct one? How can Keras know that the right one is 1 in this case and not a 28?

Let's look at the concrete example we looked in the previous chapter more in depth. Let's suppose we import the MNIST dataset with this code:

```
(X_train, y_train), (X_test, y_test) = mnist.load_data()
```

In the previous chapter, we reshaped the input tensors with

```
X_train = X_train.reshape(X_train.shape[0], 1, 28, 28).astype('float32')
```

As you will notice, we added a dimension of 1 before the x and y dimensions of 28. The 1 is the number of channels in the image: since it's a grayscale image, it has only one channel. But we could have added the number of channels also after the x and y dimensions of 28. That was our choice. We can tell Keras which dimension to take with the code that we discussed in Chapter 3:

```
K.set_image_dim_ordering('th')
```

This line is important, since Keras needs to know which one is the channel dimension in order to be able to extract the right channel dimension for the convolutional operation. Remember that for the kernels we specify only x and y dimensions, so Keras needs to find the third dimension by itself: in this case a 1. You will remember that a value of 'th' will expect the channel dimension to come before the x, y dimensions, while a value of 'tf' will expect the channel dimension to be the last one. So, it is just a matter of being consistent. You tell Keras with the code above, where the channel dimension is and then reshape your data accordingly. Let's consider a few additional examples to make the concept even clearer.

Let's suppose we consider the following network with set_image_dim_ordering('th') (we will neglect the dimension for the number of observations m) when using MNIST images as the input:

```
Input tensors shape: 1×28×28
Convolutional Layer 1 with 32 kernels, each 5×5: output shape
32×24×24
Convolutional Layer 2 with 16 kernels, each 3×3: output shape
16×22×22
```

The kernels in the second convolutional layer will have dimensions of $32 \times 3 \times 3$. The number of channels coming from the first convolutional layer (32) do not play a role in determining the dimensions of the output of the second convolutional layer, since we sum over that dimension. In fact, if we change the number of kernels in the first layer to 128, we get the following dimensions:

```
Input tensors shape: 1×28×28
Convolutional Layer 1 with 32 kernels, each 5×5: output shape
128×24×24
Convolutional Layer 2 with 16 kernels, each 3×3: output shape
16×22×22
```

As you can see, the output dimensions of the second layer have not changed at all.

Note   Keras infers automatically the channel dimensions when creating the filters, so you need to tell Keras which one is the right dimension with `set_image_dim_ordering()` and then reshape your data accordingly.

WHY A 1 × 1 CONVOLUTION REDUCES DIMENSIONALITY

In this chapter we will look at inception networks, and we will use 1×1 kernels, with the reasonsing that those reduce dimensionality. At first it seems counter-intuitive, but you need to remember from the previous section discussion, that a filter always has a third dimension. Consider the following set of layers:

```
Input tensors shape: 1 × 28 × 28
Convolutional Layer 1 with 32 kernels, each 5 × 5: output shape
128 × 24 × 24
```

```
Convolutional Layer 2 with 16 kernels, each 1 × 1: output shape
16 × 24 × 24
```

Note how the layer with 1 × 1 kernels reduces the dimensions of the previous layer. It changes the dimensions from 128 × 24 × 24 to 16 × 24 × 24. A 1 × 1 kernel will not change the x, y dimensions of the tensors but it will change the channel dimension. This is the reason why, if you read blogs or books on inception networks, you will read that those kernels are used to reduce dimensions of the tensors used.

Kernels 1 × 1 does not change the x, y dimensions of tensors, but will change the channel dimension. This is why they are often used to reduce dimensionality of the tensors flowing through a network.

History and Basics of Inception Networks

Inception networks were first proposed in a famous paper by Szegedy et al. titled *Going Deeper with Convolutions*.[1] This new architecture that we will discuss in detail is the result of the efforts to get better results in image recognition tasks without increasing the computational budget.[2] Adding more and more layers will create models with more and more parameters that will be increasingly difficult and slow to train. Additionally the authors wanted to find methods that could be used on machines that may not be as powerful as the ones used in big data centers. As they state in the paper, their models were designed to keep a "computational budget of 1.5 billion multiply-adds at inference time". It is important that inference is cheap, because then it can be done on devices that are not that powerful; for example, on mobile phones.

---

[1]The original paper can be accessed on the arXiv archive at this link: http://toe.lt/4.
[2]With computational budget we determine the time and hardware resources needed to perform a specific computation (for example, training a network).

Note that the goal of this chapter is not to analyze the entire original paper on inception networks, but to explain the new building blocks and techniques that have been used and show you how to use them in your projects. To develop inception networks, we will need to start using the functional Keras APIs, work with multiple loss functions, and perform operations on the dataset with layers that are evaluated in parallel and not sequentially. We will also not look at all variants of the architecture, because that would simply require us to list the results of a few papers and will not bring any additional value to the reader (that is better served by reading the original papers). If you are interested, the best advice I can give you is to download it and study the original paper. You will find lots of interesting information in there. But at the end of this chapter, you will have the tools to really understand those new networks and will be able to develop one with Keras.

Let's go back to "classical" CNNs. Typically, those have a standard structure: stacked convolutional layers (with pooling of course) followed by a set of dense layers. It is very tempting to just increase the number of layers or the number of kernels or their size to try to get a better result. This leads to overfitting issues and therefore requires heavy use of regularization techniques (like dropout) to try to counter this problem. Bigger sizes (both in the number of layers and kernel size and numbers) mean of course a larger number of parameters and therefore the need of increasingly high computational resources. To summarize, some of the main problems of "classical" CNNs are as follows:

- It is very difficult to get the right kernel size. Each image is different. Typically, larger kernels are good for more globally distributed information, and smaller ones for locally distributed information.

- Deep CNNs are prone to overfitting.

- Training and inference of networks with many parameters is computationally intensive.

Inception Module: Naïve Version

To overcome these difficulties, the main idea of Szegedy and the co-authors of the paper is to perform convolution with multiple-size kernels in parallel, to be able to detect features at different sizes at the same time, instead of adding convolutional layer after layer sequentially. Those kinds of networks are said to be going *wider* instead of *deeper*.

For example, we may do convolution with 1×1, 3×3 and 5×5 kernels, and even max pooling at the same time in parallel, instead of adding several convolutional layers, one after the other. In Figure 4-1, you can see how the different convolutions can be done in parallel in what is called the naïve *inception module*.

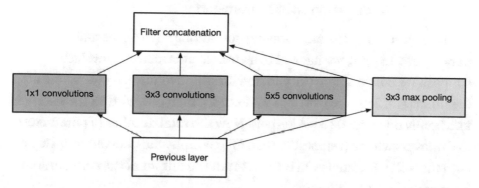

Figure 4-1. *Different convolutions with different kernel sizes done in parallel. This is the basic module used in inception networks called the inception module.*

In the example in Figure 4-1, the 1×1 kernel will look at very localized information, while the 5×5 will be able to spot more global features. In the next section, we will look at how we can develop exactly that with Keras.

Number of Parameters in the Naïve Inception Module

Let's look at the difference in number of parameters between inception and classical CNNs. Let's suppose we consider the example in Figure 4-1. Let's suppose the "previous layer" is the input layer with the MNIST dataset. For the sake of this comparison, we will use 32 kernels for all layers or convolutional operations. The number of parameters for each convolution operation in the naïve inception module is

- 1×1 convolutions: 64 parameters[3]

- 3×3 convolutions: 320 parameters

- 5×5 convolutions: 832 parameters

Remember that the max-pooling operations have no learnable parameters. In total, we have 1216 learnable parameters. Now let's suppose we create a network with the three convolutional layers, one after the other. The first one with 32 1×1 kernels, then one with 32 3×3 kernels, and finally one with 32 5×5 kernels. Now the total number of parameters in the layers will be (remember that, for example, the convolutional layer with the 32 3×3 kernels will have as input the output of the convolutional layer with the 32 1×1 kernels):

- Layer with 1×1 convolutions: 64 parameters

- Layer with 3×3 convolutions: 9248 parameters

- Layer with 5×5 convolutions: 25632 parameters

For a total of 34944 learnable parameters. Roughly 30 times the number of the parameters as the inception version. You can easily see how such parallel processing reduces drastically the number of parameters that the model must learn.

---

[3]Remember in this case we have one weight and one bias.

Inception Module with Dimension Reduction

In the naïve inception module, we get a smaller number of learnable parameters with respect to classical CNNs, but we can actually do even better. We can use 1 × 1 convolutions at the right places (mainly before the higher dimension convolutions) to reduce dimensions. This allows us to use an increasing number of such modules without blowing up the computational budget. In Figure 4-2, you can see how such a module could look.

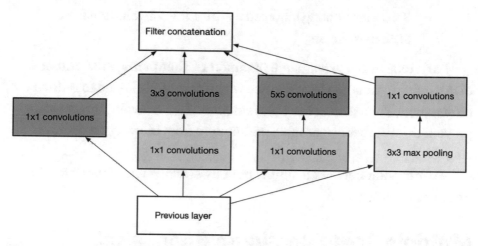

Figure 4-2.   *Inception module example with dimension reduction*

It is instructive to see how many learnable parameters we have in this module. To see where the dimensionality reduction really helps, let's suppose that the previous layer is the output of a previous operation and that its output has the dimensions of 256, 28, 28. Now let's compare the naïve module and the one with dimension reduction pictured in Figure 4-2.

Naïve module:

- 1 × 1 convolutions with 8 kernels: 2056 parameters[4]

- 3 × 3 convolutions with 8 kernels: 18440 parameters

- 5 × 5 convolutions with 8 kernels: 51208 parameters

---

[4]Remember in this case we have one weight and one bias.

For a total of 71704 learnable parameters.

Module with dimension reduction:

- 1×1 convolutions with 8 kernels: 2056 parameters

- 1×1 followed by the 3×3 convolutions: 2640 parameters

- 1×1 followed by the 5×5 convolutions: 3664 parameters

- 3×3 max pooling followed by the 1×1 convolutions: 2056 parameters

For a total of 10416 learnable parameters. Comparing the number of learnable parameters, you can see why this module is said to reduce dimensions. Thanks to a smart placement of 1×1 convolutions, we can prevent the number of learnable parameters from blowing up without control.

An inception network is simply built by stacking lots of those modules one after the other.

Multiple Cost Functions: GoogLeNet

In Figure 4-3, you can see the main structure of the GoogLeNet network that won the imagenet challenge. This network, as described in the paper referenced at the beginning, stacks several inception models one after the other. The problem is, as the authors of the original paper quickly discovered, the middle layers tend to "die". Meaning they tend to stop playing any role in the learning. To keep them from "dying," the authors introduced classifiers along the network, as depicted in Figure 4-3.

Each part of the network (PART 1, PART 2, and PART 3 in Figure 4-3) will be trained as a stand-alone classifier. The training of the three parts does not happen independently, but at the same time, in a very similar way to what happens in multi-task learning (MTL).

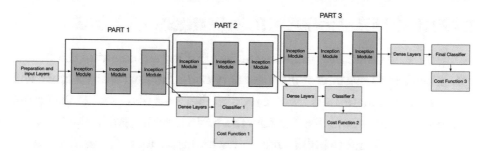

Figure 4-3. *The high-level architecture of the GoogLeNet network*

To prevent the middle part of the network from not being so effective and effectively dying out, the authors introduced two classifiers along the network, indicated in Figure 4-3 with the yellow boxes. They introduced two intermediate loss functions and then computed the total loss function as a weighted sum of the auxiliary losses, effectively using a total loss evaluated with this formula:

```
Total Loss = Cost Function 1 + 0.3 * (Cost Function 2) + 0.3 *
(Cost Function 3)
```

Where `Cost Function` 1 is the cost function evaluated with PART 1, `Cost Function` 2 is evaluated with PART 2, and `Cost Function` 3 with PART 3. Testing has shown that this is quite effective and you get a much better result than simply training the entire network as a single classifier. Of course, the auxiliary losses are used only in training and not during inference.

The authors have developed several versions of inception networks, with increasingly complex modules. If you are interested, you should read the original papers as they are very instructive. A second paper with more a complex architecture by the authors can be found at `https://arxiv.org/pdf/1512.00567v3.pdf`.

Example of Inception Modules in Keras

Using the functional APIs of Keras makes building an inception module extremely easy. Let's look at the necessary code. For space reasons, we will not build a complete model with a dataset, because that would take up too much space and would distract from the main learning goal, which is to see how to use Keras to build a network with layers that are evaluated in parallel instead of sequentially.

Let's suppose for the sake of this example that our training dataset is the CIFAR10.[5] This is made of images, all 32 × 32 with three channels (the images are in color). So first we need to define the input layer of our network:

```
from keras.layers import Input
input_img = Input(shape = (32, 32, 3))
```

Then we simply define one layer after the other:

```
from keras.layers import Conv2D, MaxPooling2D
tower_1 = Conv2D(64, (1,1), padding='same', activation='relu')
(input_img)
tower_1 = Conv2D(64, (3,3), padding='same', activation='relu')
(tower_1)
tower_2 = Conv2D(64, (1,1), padding='same', activation='relu')
(input_img)
tower_2 = Conv2D(64, (5,5), padding='same', activation='relu')
(tower_2)
tower_3 = MaxPooling2D((3,3), strides=(1,1), padding='same')
(input_img)
tower_3 = Conv2D(64, (1,1), padding='same', activation='relu')
(tower_3)
```

---

[5]You can find all information on the dataset at https://www.cs.toronto. edu/~kriz/cifar.html.

This code will build the module depicted in Figure 4-4. The Keras functional APIs are easy to use: you define the layers as functions of another layer. Each function returns a tensor of the appropriate dimensions. The nice thing is that you don't have to worry about dimensions; you can simply define layer after layer. Just take care to use the right one for the input. For example, with this line:

```
tower_1 = Conv2D(64, (1,1), padding='same', activation='relu')
(input_img)
```

You define a tensor, named tower_1, that is evaluated after a convolutional operation with the input_img tensor and 64 1 × 1 kernels. Then this line:

```
tower_1 = Conv2D(64, (3,3), padding='same', activation='relu')
(tower_1)
```

Defines a new tensor that is obtained by the convolution of 64 3 × 3 kernels with the output of the previous line. We have taken the input tensor, performed convolution with 64 1 × 1 kernels, and then performed convolution with 64 3 × 3 kernels again.

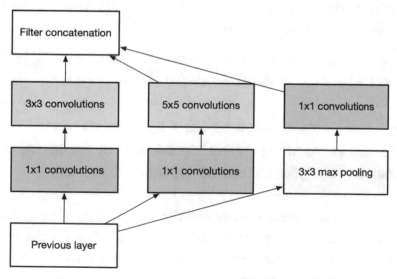

Figure 4-4. The inception module built from the given code

The concatenation of the layers is easy:

```
from keras.layers import concatenate
from tensorflow.keras import optimizers
output = concatenate([tower_1, tower_2, tower_3], axis = 3)
```

Now let's add the couple of necessary dense layers:

```
from keras.layers import Flatten, Dense
output = Flatten()(output)
out     = Dense(10, activation='softmax')(output)
```

Then we finally create the model:

```
from keras.models import Model
model = Model(inputs = input_img, outputs = out)
```

This model can then be compiled and trained as usual. An example of usage could be

```
epochs = 50
model.compile(loss='categorical_crossentropy',
optimizer=optimizers.Adam(), metrics=['accuracy'])
model.fit(X_train, y_train, validation_data=(X_test, y_test),
epochs=epochs, batch_size=32)
```

Supposing the training dataset is composed by the arrays (X_train and y_train) and the validation dataset by (X_test, y_test).

Note   In all convolutional operations in the inception module, you have to use the `padding='same'` option, since all the outputs of the convolutional operations must have the same dimensions.

This section gave you a brief introduction to how to develop more complex network architectures using the functional APIs of Keras. You should now have a basic understanding of how inception networks work and their basic building blocks.

Digression: Custom Losses in Keras

Sometimes it is useful to be able to develop custom losses in Keras. From the official Keras documentation (https://keras.io/losses/):

> *You can either pass the name of an existing loss function or pass a TensorFlow/Theano symbolic function that returns a scalar for each data point and takes the following two arguments:*
>
> *y_true: True labels. TensorFlow/Theano tensor.*
>
> *y_pred: Predictions. TensorFlow/Theano tensor of the same shape as y_true.*

Let's suppose we want to define a loss that calculates the average of the predictions. We would need to write this

```
import keras.backend as K
def mean_predictions(y_true, y_pred):
    return K.mean(y_pred)
```

And then we can simply use it in the compile call as follows:

```
model.compile(optimizer='rmsprop',
             loss=mean_predictions,
             metrics=['accuracy'])
```

Although this would not make so much sense as a loss. Now this starts to get interesting the moment where the loss function can be evaluated only using intermediate results from specific layers. But to do that, we need to use a small trick. Since, as per official documentation, the function can only accept as input true labels and predictions. To do this we need to create a function that return a function that accepts only the true labels and the predictions. Seems convoluted? Let's look at an example to understand it. Let's suppose we have this model:

```
inputs = Input(shape=(512,))
x1 = Dense(128, activation=sigmoid)(inputs)
x2 = Dense(64, activation=sigmoid)(x1)
predictions = Dense(10, activation='softmax')(x2)
model = Model(inputs=inputs, outputs=predictions)
```

We can define a loss function that depends on x1 with this code[6] (what the loss is doing is not relevant):

```
def custom_loss(layer):
    def loss(y_true,y_pred):
        return K.mean(K.square(y_pred - y_true) +
        K.square(layer), axis=-1)
    return loss
```

Then we can simply use the loss function as before:

```
model.compile(optimizer='adam',
            loss=custom_loss(x1),
            metrics=['accuracy'])
```

This is an easy way to develop and use custom losses. It is also sometimes useful to be able to train a model with multiple losses, as described in the inception networks. Keras is ready for this. Once you define the loss functions you can use the following syntax

```
model.compile(loss = [loss1,loss2], loss_weights = [l1,l2], ...)
```

and Keras will then use as loss function

```
l1*loss1+l2*loss2
```

---

[6]The code was inspired by http://toe.lt/7.

Consider that each loss will only affect the weights that are on the path between the inputs and the loss functions. In Figure 4-5, you can see a network divided in different parts: A, B, and C. `loss1` is calculated using the output of B, and `loss2` of C. Therefore, `loss1` will only affect the weights in A and B, while `loss2` will affect weights in A, B and C, as you can see in Figure 4-5.

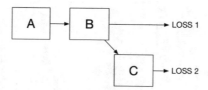

Figure 4-5. *A schematic representation of the influence of multiple loss functions on different network parts*

As a side note, this technique is heavily used in what is called *multi-task learning* (MTL).[7]

How To Use Pre-Trained Networks

Keras makes pre-trained deep learning models available for you to use. The models, called *applications*, can be used for predictions on new data. The models have already been trained on big datasets, so there is no need for big datasets or long training sessions. You can find all applications information on the official documentation at `https://keras.io/applications/`. At the moment of writing there are 20 models available, each a variation of one of the following:

- Xception

- VGG16

---

[7]You can find more information at `https://en.wikipedia.org/wiki/Multi-task_learning`

- VGG19

- ResNet

- ResNetV2

- ResNeXt

- InceptionV3

- InceptionResNetV2

- MobileNet

- MobileNetV2

- DenseNEt

- NASNet

Let's look at one example, and while doing so, let's discuss the different parameters used in the functions. The pre-ready models are all in the keras.applications package. Each model has its own package. For example, ResNet50 is in the keras.applications.resnet50. Let's suppose we have one image we want to classify. We may use the VGG16 network, a well known network that is very successful in image recognition. We can start with the following code

```
import tensorflow as tf
from tensorflow.keras.applications.vgg16 import VGG16
from tensorflow.keras.preprocessing import image
from tensorflow.keras.applications.vgg16 import preprocess_
input , decode_predictions

import numpy as np
```

Then we can simply load the model with a simple line

```
model = VGG16(weights='imagenet')
```

The weights parameter is very important. If weights is None the weights are randomly initialized. That means that you get the VGG16 architecture and you can train it yourself. But be aware, it has roughly 138 million parameters, so you will need a really big training dataset and lots of patience (and a really powerful hardware). If you use the value imagenet, the weights are the ones obtained by training the network with the imagenet dataset.[8] If you want a pre-trained network, you should use weights = 'imagenet'.

If you get an error message about certificates and you are on a Mac, there is an easy solution. The command above will try to download the weights over SSL and, if you just installed Python from python.org, the installed certificates will not work on your machine. Simply open a Finder window, navigate to the Applications/Python 3.7 (or the Python version you have installed), and double-click Install Certificates.command. A Terminal window will open, and a script will run. After that, the VGG16() call will work without an error message.

After that, we need to tell Keras where the image is (let's suppose you have it in the folder where the Jupyter Notebook is) and load it:

```
img_path = 'elephant.jpg'
img = image.load_img(img_path, target_size = (224, 224))
```

You can find the image in the GitHub repository in the folder for Chapter 4. After that we need

```
x = image.img_to_array(img)
x = np.expand_dims(x, axis=0)
x = preprocess_input(x)
```

First, you convert the image to an array, then you need to expand its dimensions. What is meant is the following: the model works with batches

---

[8]http://www.image-net.org

of images, meaning it will expect as input a tensor with four axes (*index in the batch of images, resolution along x, resolution along y, number of channels*). But our image has only three dimensions, the horizontal and vertical resolutions and the number of channels (in our example three, for the RGB channels). We need to add one dimension for the *samples* dimension. To be more concrete, our image has dimensions (224,244,3), but the model expects a tensor of dimensions (1,224,224,3), so we need to add the first dimension.

This can be done with the numpy function expand_dims(), which simply inserts a new axis in the tensor.[9] As a last step, you need to pre-process the input image, since each model expects something slightly different (normalized between +1 and -1, or between 0 and 1, and so on) with the preprocess_input(x) call.

Now we are ready to let the model predict the class of the image with the following:

```
preds = model.predict(x)
```

To get the top three classes of the prediction, we can use the decode_predictions() function.

```
print('Predicted:', decode_predictions(preds, top=3)[0])
```

It will produce (with our image) the following predictions:

```
Predicted: [('n02504013', 'Indian_elephant', 0.7278206),
('n02504458', 'African_elephant', 0.14308284), ('n01871265',
'tusker', 0.12798567)]
```

The decode_predictions() returns tuples in the form (class_name, class_description, score). The first cryptic string is the internal class name, the second is the description (what we are interested in), and the last one is the probability. It seems our image, according to the VGG16

---

[9]You can check the official documentation for the function at http://toe.lt/5.

network, is with 72.8% probability an Indian elephant. I am not an expert on elephants, but I will trust the model. To use a different pre-trained network (for example ResNet50), you need to change the following imports:

```
from keras.applications.resnet50 import ResNet50
from keras.applications.resnet50 import preprocess_input,
decode_predictions
```

And the way you define the model:

```
model = ResNet50(weights='imagenet')
```

The rest of the code remains the same.

Transfer Learning: An Introduction

Transfer learning is a technique where a model trained to solve a specific problem is re-purposed[10] for a new challenge related to the first problem. Let's suppose we have a network with many layers. In image recognition typically, the first layers will learn to detect generic features, and the last layers will be able to detect more specific ones.[11] Remember that in a classification problem the last layer will have N softmax neurons (assuming we are classifiying N classes), and therefore must learn to be very specific to your problem. You can intuitively understand transfer learning with the following steps, where we introduce some notation we will use in the next sections and chapters. Let's suppose we have a network with n_L layers.

---

[10]The term has been used by Yosinki in https://arxiv.org/abs/1411.1792.

[11]You can find a very interesting paper on the subject by Yosinki et al. at https://arxiv.org/abs/1411.1792.

1. We train a *base network* (or get a pre-trained model) on a big dataset (called a *base dataset*) related to our problem. For example, if we want to classify dogs' images, we may train a model in this step on the imagenet dataset (since we basically want to classify images). It is important that, at this step, the dataset has enough data and that the task is related to the problem we want to solve. Getting a network trained for speech recognition will not be good at dog images classification. This network will probably not be that good for your specific problem.

2. We get a new dataset that we call a *target dataset* (for example, dogs' breeds images) that will be our new training dataset. Typically, this dataset will be much smaller than the one used in Step 1.

3. You then train a new network, called *target network*, on the *target dataset*. The target network will typically have the same first n_k (with $n_k < n_L$) layers of our base network. The learnable parameters of the first layers (let's say 1 to n_k, with $n_k < n_L$) are inherited from the base network trained in Step 1, and are not changed during the training of the target network. Only the last and new layers (in our example from layer n_K to n_L) are trained. The idea is that layers from 1 to n_k (from the base network) will learn enough features in Step 1 to distinguish dogs from other animals, and the layers n_k to n_L (in the target network) will learn the features needed to distinguish different breeds. Sometimes you can even train your entire target network using the weights inherited from the base network as the initial values of the weights, although this requires much more powerful hardware.

Note   If the target dataset is small, the best strategy is to keep the layers inherited from the base network frozen, since otherwise it's very easy to overfit the small dataset.

The idea behind this is that you hope that in Step 1, the base network has learned to extract generic features from images well enough and therefore you want to use this learned knowledge and avoid the need to learn it again. But to make predictions better, you want to fine-tune the predictions of your network for your specific case, optimizing how your target network extracts specific features (that typically happens in the last layers of a network) that are related to your problem.

In other words, you can think it this way. To recognize dog breeds, you implicitly follow these steps:

1.   You look at an image and decide if it's a dog or not.

2.   If you are looking at a dog, you classify it into broad classes (for example, terrier).

3.   After that, you classify into sub-classes (for example, a Welsh terrier or Tibetan terrier).

Transfer learning is based on the idea that Steps 1 and possibly 2 can be learned from a lot of generic images (for example from the imagenet dataset) from a base network, and that Step 3 can be learned by a much smaller dataset with the help of what has been learned in Step 1 and 2.

When the target dataset is much smaller than the base dataset, this is a very powerful tool that will help avoiding overfitting of your training dataset.

This method is very useful when used with pre-trained models. For example, using a VGG16 network trained on imagenet, and then re-training just the last layers is typically an extremely efficient way to solve specific image recognition problems. You get lots of features detection capabilities for free. Keep in mind that training such networks on the imagenet networks costs several thousands of GPU hours. It's typically not doable for researchers without the needed hardware and know-how. In the next sections, we will look at how to do exactly that. With Keras, it's really easy and it will allow you to solve image classification problems with an accuracy that would not otherwise be possible. In Figure 4-6, you can see a schematic representation of the transfer learning process.

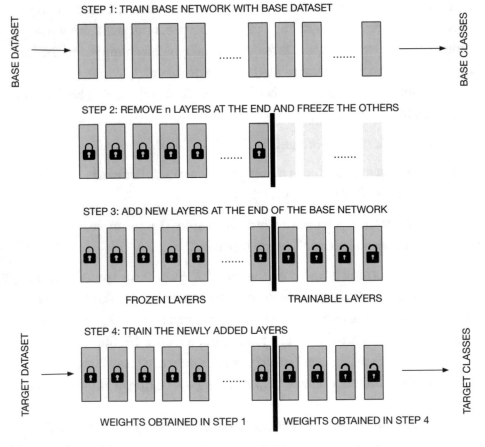

Figure 4-6. *A schematic representation of the transfer learning process*

A Dog and Cat Problem

The best way to understand how transfer learning works in practice is to try it in practice. Our goal is to be able to classify images of dogs and cats as best as we can, with the least effort (in computational resources) as possible. To do that, we will use the dataset with dog and cat images that you can find on Kaggle at `https://www.kaggle.com/c/dogs-vs-cats`. Warning: The download is almost 800MB. In Figure 4-7, you can see some of the images we will have to classify.

Figure 4-7. *Random samples of the images contained in the dog versus cat dataset*

Classical Approach to Transfer Learning

The naïve way of solving this problem is to create a CNN model and train it with the images. First of all, we need to load the images and resize them to make sure they all have the same resolution. If you check the images in the dataset, you will notice that each has a different resolution. To do that let's resize all the images to (150, 150) pixels. In Python, we would use this:

```python
import glob
import numpy as np
import os

img_res = (150, 150)

train_files = glob.glob('training_data/*')
train_imgs = [img_to_array(load_img(img, target_size=img_res))
for img in train_files]
train_imgs = np.array(train_imgs)
train_labels = [fn.split('/')[1].split('.')[0].strip() for fn
in train_files]

validation_files = glob.glob('validation_data/*')
validation_imgs = [img_to_array(load_img(img, target_size=img_
res)) for img in validation_files]
validation_imgs = np.array(validation_imgs)
validation_labels = [fn.split('/')[1].split('.')[0].strip() for
fn in validation_files]
```

Supposing we have 3000 training images in a folder called training_ data and 1000 validation images in a folder called validation_data, the shapes of the train_imgs and validation_imgs will be as follows:

```
(3000, 150, 150, 3)
(1000, 150, 150, 3)
```

As usual we will need to normalize the images. Each pixel now has a value between 0 and 255 and is an integer. So first we convert the numbers to floating point, and then we normalize them by dividing by 255, so that each value is now between 0 and 1.

```
train_imgs_scaled = train_imgs.astype('float32')
validation_imgs_scaled  = validation_imgs.astype('float32')
train_imgs_scaled /= 255
validation_imgs_scaled /= 255
```

If you check the train_labels you will see that they are strings: 'dog' or 'cat'. We need to transform the labels to integers, in particular into 0 and 1. To do that, we can use the Keras function called LabelEncoder.

```
from sklearn.preprocessing import LabelEncoder
le = LabelEncoder()
le.fit(train_labels)
train_labels_enc = le.transform(train_labels)
validation_labels_enc = le.transform(validation_labels)
```

We can check the labels with this code:

```
print(train_labels[10:15], train_labels_enc[10:15])
```

Which will give this:

```
['cat', 'dog', 'cat', 'cat', 'dog'] [0 1 0 0 1]
```

Now we are ready to build our model. We can do this easily with the following code:

```
from tensorflow.keras.layers import Conv2D, MaxPooling2D,
Flatten, Dense, Dropout
from tensorflow.keras.models import Sequential
from tensorflow.keras import optimizers
```

```
model = Sequential()
model.add(Conv2D(16, kernel_size=(3, 3), activation='relu',
                input_shape=input_shape))
model.add(MaxPooling2D(pool_size=(2, 2)))

model.add(Conv2D(64, kernel_size=(3, 3), activation='relu'))
model.add(MaxPooling2D(pool_size=(2, 2)))

model.add(Conv2D(128, kernel_size=(3, 3), activation='relu'))
model.add(MaxPooling2D(pool_size=(2, 2)))

model.add(Flatten())
model.add(Dense(512, activation='relu'))
model.add(Dense(1, activation='sigmoid'))

model.compile(loss='binary_crossentropy',
                optimizer=optimizers.RMSprop(),
                metrics=['accuracy'])
```

This is a small network that has this structure:

Layer (type)	Output Shape	Param #
conv2d_3 (Conv2D)	(None, 148, 148, 16)	448
max_pooling2d_3 (MaxPooling2	(None, 74, 74, 16)	0
conv2d_4 (Conv2D)	(None, 72, 72, 64)	9280
max_pooling2d_4 (MaxPooling2	(None, 36, 36, 64)	0
conv2d_5 (Conv2D)	(None, 34, 34, 128)	73856
max_pooling2d_5 (MaxPooling2	(None, 17, 17, 128)	0
flatten_1 (Flatten)	(None, 36992)	0
dense_2 (Dense)	(None, 512)	18940416
dense_3 (Dense)	(None, 1)	513

Total params: 19,024,513
Trainable params: 19,024,513
Non-trainable params: 0

In Figure 4-8, you can see a schematic representation of the network to give you an idea of the layer sequence.

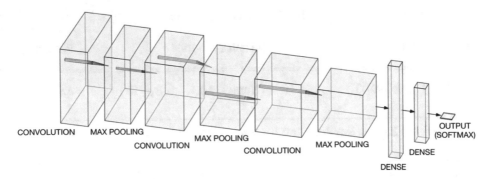

CONVOLUTION   MAX POOLING   CONVOLUTION   MAX POOLING   CONVOLUTION   MAX POOLING   DENSE   DENSE   OUTPUT (SOFTMAX)

Figure 4-8. *A schematic representation of the network to give you an idea of the layer sequence*

At this point we can train the network with the following:

```
batch_size = 30
num_classes = 2
epochs = 2
input_shape = (150, 150, 3)
model.fit(x=train_imgs_scaled, y=train_labels_enc,
                  validation_data=(validation_imgs_scaled,
                  validation_labels_enc),
                  batch_size=batch_size,
                  epochs=epochs,
                  verbose=1)
```

With two epochs, we get to about 69% validation accuracy and 70% training accuracy. Not really a good result. Let's see if we can do better than this in just two epochs. The reason to do this in two epochs is merely a way of checking quickly different possibilities. Training such networks for many epochs can take easily few hours. Note that this model overfit the training data. That becomes clearly visible when training for more epochs, but the main goal here is not to get the best model, but to see how you can use pre-trained model to get better results, so we will ignore this problem.

Now let's import the VGG16 pre-trained network.

```
from tensorflow.keras.applications import vgg16
from tensorflow.keras.models import Model
import tensorflow.keras as keras

base_model=vgg16.VGG16(include_top=False, weights='imagenet')
```

Note that the include_top=False parameter removes the last three fully connected layers of the network. In this way, we can append our own layers to the base network with the code:

```
from tensorflow.keras.layers import
Dense,GlobalAveragePooling2D
x=base_model.output
x=GlobalAveragePooling2D()(x)
x=Dense(1024,activation='relu')(x)
preds=Dense(1,activation='softmax')(x)
model=Model(inputs=base_model.input,outputs=preds)
```

We added a pooling layer, then a Dense layer with 1024 neurons, and then an output layer with one neuron with a softmax activation function to do binary classification. We can check the structure with the following:

```
model.summary()
```

The output is quite long, but at the end you will find this:

```
Total params: 15,242,050
Trainable params: 15,242,050
Non-trainable params: 0
```

All the 22 layers are trainable at the moment. To be able to really do transfer learning, we need to freeze all layers of the VGG16 base network. To do that we can do the following:

```
for layer in model.layers[:20]:
    layer.trainable=False
for layer in model.layers[20:]:
    layer.trainable=True
```

This code will set the first 20 layers to a non trainable status, and the last two to a trainable status. Then we can compile our model as follows:

```
model.compile(optimizer='Adam',loss='sparse_categorical_crossen
tropy',metrics=['accuracy'])
```

Note that we used loss='sparse_categorical_crossentropy' to be able to use the labels as they are, without having to hot-encode them. As we have done before, we can now train the network:

```
model.fit(x=train_imgs_scaled, y=train_labels_enc,
                    validation_data=(validation_imgs_scaled,
                    validation_labels_enc),
                    batch_size=batch_size,
                    epochs=epochs,
                    verbose=1)
```

Note that although we are training only a portion of the network, this will require much more time than the simple network we tried before. The result will be an astounding 88% in two epochs. An incredibly better result than before! Your output should look something like this:

```
Train on 3000 samples, validate on 1000 samples
Epoch 1/2
3000/3000 [==============================] - 283s 94ms/sample -
loss: 0.3563 - acc: 0.8353 - val_loss: 0.2892 - val_acc: 0.8740
```

```
Epoch 2/2
3000/3000 [==============================] - 276s 92ms/sample -
loss: 0.2913 - acc: 0.8730 - val_loss: 0.2699 - val_acc: 0.8820
```

This was thanks to the pre-trained first layers, which saved us a lot of work.

Experimentation with Transfer Learning

What if we want to try different architectures for the target networks, and we want to add a few more layers and try again? The previous approach has a slight downside: we need to train the entire network each time event though only the last layers should be trained. As you see from the section above, one epoch took roughly 4.5 minutes. Can we be more efficient? Turns out we can.

Consider the configuration depicted in Figure 4-9.

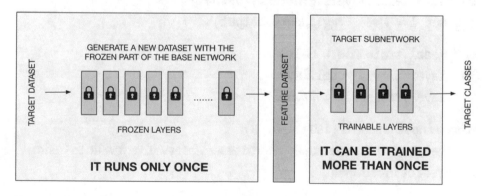

Figure 4-9. *A schematic representation of a more flexible way of doing transfer learning in practice*

The idea is to generate a new dataset that we will call the *feature dataset,* with the frozen layers. Since they will not be changed by training, those layers will always generate the same output. We can use this feature dataset as new input for a much smaller network (that we will call the *target subnetwork*), made by only the new layers we added to the base layer in the previous section. We will need to train only a few layers, and that will be much faster. The generation of the feature dataset will take some time, but this must be done only once. At this point you can test different architecture for the target subnetwork and find the best configuration for your problem. Let's see how we can do that in Keras. The base dataset preparation is the same as before, so we will not do it again.

Let's import the VGG16 pre-trained network as before:

```
from tensorflow.keras.applications import vgg16
from tensorflow.keras.models import Model
import tensorflow.keras as keras

vgg = vgg16.VGG16(include_top=False, weights='imagenet',
                                    input_shape=input_shape)

output = vgg.layers[-1].output
output = keras.layers.Flatten()(output)
vgg_model = Model(vgg.input, output)

vgg_model.trainable = False
for layer in vgg_model.layers:
    layer.trainable = False
```

where input_shape is (150, 150, 3).

We can simply generate the features dataset with a few lines (using the predict functionality):

```
def get_ features(model, input_imgs):
    features = model.predict(input_imgs, verbose=0)
    return features

train_features_vgg = get_features(vgg_model, train_imgs_scaled)
validation_features_vgg = get_features(vgg_model, validation_
imgs_scaled)
```

Note that this will take a few minutes on a modern laptop. On a modern MacBook Pro, this will take 40 CPU minutes, meaning that if you have more cores/threads it will take a fraction of it. On my laptop, it takes effectively four minutes. Remember that since we used the parameter `include_top = False`, the three dense layers at the end of the network have been removed. The `train_features_vgg` will contain just the output of the last layer of the base network without the last three dense layers. At this point we can simply build our target subnetwork:

```
from tensorflow.keras.layers import Conv2D, MaxPooling2D,
Flatten, Dense, Dropout, InputLayer
from tensorflow.keras.models import Sequential
from tensorflow.keras import optimizers

input_shape = vgg_model.output_shape[1]


model = Sequential()
model.add(InputLayer(input_shape=(input_shape,)))
model.add(Dense(512, activation='relu', input_dim=input_shape))
model.add(Dropout(0.3))
model.add(Dense(512, activation='relu'))
model.add(Dropout(0.3))
model.add(Dense(1, activation='sigmoid'))

model.compile(loss='binary_crossentropy',
              optimizer=optimizers.Adam(lr =1e-4),
              metrics=['accuracy'])

model.summary()
```

Training this network will be much faster than before. You will get in the range of 90% accuracy in a few seconds' time (remember that you have created a new training dataset this time). But now you can change this network and it will be much faster to test different architectures. This time, one epoch takes only six seconds, in comparison to the 4.5 minutes in the previous example. This method is much more efficient than the previous one. We split the training in two phases:

1. Creation of the feature dataset. Done only once. (In our example, this needs about four minutes.)

2. Train the new layers as a stand-alone network, using the feature dataset as input. (This takes six seconds for each epoch.)

If we want to train our network for 100 epochs, with this method we would need 14 minutes. With the method described in the previous section, we would need 7.5 hours! The downside is that you need to create the new feature dataset for each dataset you want to use. In our example, we needed to do it for the training and for the validation dataset.

CHAPTER 5

Cost Functions and Style Transfer

In this chapter we will look in more depth at the role of the cost function in neural network models. In particular, we will discuss the MSE (mean square error) and the cross-entropy and discuss their origin and their interpretation. We will look at why we can use them to solve problems and how the MSE can be interpreted in a statistical sense, as well as how cross-entropy is related to information theory. Then, to give you an example of a much more advanced use of special loss functions, we will learn how to do neural style transfer, where we will discuss a neural network to paint in the style of famous painters.

Components of a Neural Network Model

At this point you have seen and developed several models that try to solve different types of problems. You should know by now that in all the neural network models, there are (at least) three main building blocks:

- Network architecture (number of layers, type of layers, activation functions, etc.)

- Loss function (MSE, cross-entropy, etc.)

- The optimizer

© Umberto Michelucci 2019
U. Michelucci, *Advanced Applied Deep Learning*,
https://doi.org/10.1007/978-1-4842-4976-5_5

The optimizer is not typically problem specific. For example, to solve a regression or classification problem, you need to choose a different architecture and loss function, but you can use in both cases the same optimizer. In regression, you may use a feed-forward network and the MSE for the loss function. In classification, you may choose a convolutional neural network and the cross-entropy loss function. But in both you can use the Adam optimizer. The component that plays the biggest role in deciding what a network can learn is the loss function. Change it and you will change what your network will be able to predict and learn.

Training Seen as an Optimization Problem

Let's try to understand why this is the case in more detail. From a purely theoretical point of view, training a network means nothing more than solving a really complex optimization problem. The standard formulation of continuous optimization problem is to find the minimum of a given function

$$\min_x f(x)$$

Subject to two constraint types

$$g_i(x) \leq 0, \quad i = 1, \ldots, m$$
$$p_j(x) = 0, \quad j = 1, \ldots, n$$

where $f: \mathbb{R}^n \to \mathbb{R}$ is the continuous function we want to minimize, $g_i(x) \leq 0$ refers to the inequalities constraints, $p_j(x) = 0$ refers to the equality constraints, and $m, n \in \mathbb{N}^+$. And of course, is possible to have a problem without constraints. But how does this relate to neural networks? Well, the following parallels can be drawn:

- The function $f(x)$ is the loss function that we have chosen when building the neural network model.

- The input $x \in \mathbb{R}^n$ are the weights (the learnable parameters) of our network. Remember that any loss function that we may choose is always a function of the output of the network (that we indicate with $\hat{y}$), and the output is always a function of the weights W (the learnable parameters of the network).

When we are training a network, we are actually solving an optimization problem, one where we want to minimize the loss function with respect to the weights. We implicitly have constraints, although we normally don't declare them explicitly. For example, we may have the constraint that we want the inference time needed for one observation to be less than 10ms. In this case we would have $n = 0$ (no equality constraints), $m = 1$ (one inequality constraint) with g_1 being the inference running time. To cite Wikipedia[1]:

A loss function or cost function is a function that maps an event or values of one or more variables onto a real number intuitively representing some "cost" associated with the event

Typically, a loss function measures how bad your model understands your data. Let's look at a few simple examples so that you can understand in a concrete case this formulation of the training of a network.

---

[1]https://en.wikipedia.org/wiki/Loss_function

A Concrete Example: Linear Regression

As you know, you can perform linear regression with a network with just one neuron if you choose as its activation function the identity function[2]. We indicate the set of observations with $x^{[i]} \in \mathbb{R}^n$ with $i = 1, ..., m$ where m is the number of observations we have at our disposal. The neuron (and therefore the network) will have the output

$$\hat{y}^{[i]} = \sum_{k=1}^{n} w_k x_k^{[i]} + b$$

where we have indicated the weights with $w = (w_1, ... w_n)$. We can choose the loss function as the mean square error (MSE):

$$J(w,b) = \frac{1}{m} \sum_{k=1}^{m} \left(\hat{y}^{[i]} - y^{[i]} \right)^2$$

Where $y^{[i]}$ is the target variable that we want to predict for the ith observation. It's easy to see how the loss function that we have defined is a function of the weights and the bias. In fact, we have

$$J(w,b) = \frac{1}{m} \sum_{i=1}^{m} \left(\hat{y}^{[i]} - y^{[i]} \right)^2 = \frac{1}{m} \sum_{i=1}^{m} \left(\sum_{k=1}^{n} w_k x_k^{[i]} + b - y^{[i]} \right)^2$$

Training this network as we typically do with (for example) a gradient descent algorithm is nothing more than solving an unconstrained

---

[2]This example is discussed in detail in Michelucci, Umberto, 2018. *Applied Deep Learning: A Case-Based Approach To Understanding Deep Neural Networks.* 1. Auflage. New York: Apress. ISBN 978-1-4842-3789-2. Available from: https:// doi.org/10.1007/978-1-4842-3790-8

optimization problem where we have (using the notation we have used at the beginning):

$$f := J$$

The Cost Function
Mathematical Notation

Let's define some notation that we will use in the next sections. We will use

$\hat{y}^{[i]} \in \mathbb{R}^k$ is the output of the network for the ith observation.

$\hat{Y} \in \mathbb{R}^{m \times k}$ is the tensor containing the output of the network for all observations.[3]

$x^{[i]} \in \mathbb{R}^{n_x \times n_y \times n_c}$ represents the ith observation input features (in general, for images we would have n_c channels, and a resolution of $n_x \times n_y$).

$X \in \mathbb{R}^{m \times n_x \times n_y \times n_c}$ is the tensor containing all input observations.

W is the set of all learnable parameters that are used in the network (including the biases).

m is the number of observations.

n_c is the number of image channels (for RGB images it would be 3).

n_x is the horizontal resolution of the input images.

n_y is the vertical resolution of the input images.

J is the cost function.

In general, we will define the so-called cost (or loss) function J generically as follows:

$$J\left(X, \hat{Y}(W)\right)$$

---

[3]Remember that the order of the dimensions depends on how you structure your network and you may need to change it. The dimensions here are for illustrative purposes only.

This function, in addition to the network architecture, will define what kind of problem our neural network model will be able to solve. Note how this function

- Depends on the network architecture, since it depends on the network output $\hat{Y}$ (and therefore from the learnable parameters, W)

- Depends on the input dataset, since it depends on the input X

This is the function that will be used when finding the best weights. In almost all optimizers, the weights are updated using $\nabla_{\mathrm{w}} J\left(X, \hat{Y}(\mathrm{W})\right)$ in some form.

Typical Cost Functions

There are several cost functions that you may use when training neural networks, as we have seen in the previous chapters. In the next sections, we will look at two of the most used in detail and try to understand their meaning and origin.

Mean Square Error

The mean square error function

$$J(w,b) = \frac{1}{m} \sum_{k=1}^{m} \left(\hat{y}^{[i]} - y^{[i]} \right)^2$$

is probably the most used cost function used when developing models for regression. There are several interpretations of this cost function, but the following two should help you in get an intuitive and a more formal understanding of it.

Intuitive Explanation

J is nothing more than the average of the squared difference between the predictions and the measured values. So basically, it measures how far the predictions are from the expected values. A perfect model that would predict the data perfectly ($\hat{y}^{[i]} = y^{[i]}$ for all $i = 1, ..., m$) would have $J = 0$. In general, it holds the smallest J the better the predictions are.

Note   In general, it holds that the smaller the MSE, the better the predictions are (and therefore, the better the model is).

Minimizing the MSE means finding the parameters so that our network will give output as close as possible to our training data. Note that you could achieve a similar result by using, for example, the MAE (Mean Absolute Error) given by

$$MAE = \frac{1}{m}\sum_{k=1}^{m}\left|\hat{y}^{[i]} - y^{[i]}\right|$$

Although this is not usually done.

MSE as the Second Moment of a Moment-Generating Function

There is a more formal way of interpreting the MSE. Let's define the quantity

$$\Delta Y^{[i]} = \hat{y}^{[i]} - y^{[i]}$$

Let's define the moment-generating function

$$M_{\Delta Y}(t) := E\left[e^{t\Delta Y}\right]$$

Where we have $t \in \mathbb{R}$ and we have indicated with $E[\cdot]$ the expected value of the variable over all observations. We will skip the discussion about the existence of the expected value, depending on the characteristics of ΔY, since this goes beyond the scope of this book. We can expand $e^{t\Delta Y}$ with a Taylor series expansion[4] (we will assume we can do that):

$$e^{t\Delta Y} = 1 + t\Delta Y + \frac{t^2 \Delta Y^2}{2!} + \cdots$$

Therefore

$$M_{\Delta Y}(t) := E\left[e^{t\Delta Y}\right] = 1 + tE[\Delta Y] + \frac{t^2 E\left[\Delta Y^2\right]}{2!} + \cdots$$

$E[\Delta Y^n]$ is called the nth moment of the function $M_{\Delta Y}(t)$. You can see that the moments can be easily interpreted (at least the first):

- $E[\Delta Y]$: First moment of $M_{\Delta Y}(t)$ - *Average of* ΔY

- $E[\Delta Y^2]$: Second moment of $M_{\Delta Y}(t)$ - *is what we defined as the MSE function*

- $E[\Delta Y^3]$: Third moment of $M_{\Delta Y}(t)$ - *Skeweness*[5]

- $E[\Delta Y^4]$: Fourth moment of $M_{\Delta Y}(t)$ - *Kurtosis*[6]

We can simply write the second moment as the average over the observations

$$E\left[\Delta Y^2\right] := \frac{1}{m}\sum_{k=1}^{m}\Delta Y^{[i]2} = \frac{1}{m}\sum_{k=1}^{m}\left(\hat{y}^{[i]} - y^{[i]}\right)^2$$

---

[4]https://en.wikipedia.org/wiki/Taylor_series
[5]https://en.m.wikipedia.org/wiki/Skewness. In the case of $E[\Delta Y] = 0$.
[6]https://en.m.wikipedia.org/wiki/Kurtosis. In the case of $E[\Delta Y] = 0$.

If we assume that our model predict data with $E[\Delta Y] = 0$, then the $E[\Delta Y^2]$ (and therefore the MSE) is nothing more than the variance of the distribution of our data points $\Delta Y^{[i]}$. In this case, it simply measures how broad our points are spread around the average (that is zero): the perfect prediction. Remember that, if for an observation, we have $\Delta Y^{[i]} = 0$, it means we have $\hat{y}^{[i]} = y^{[i]}$, meaning the prediciton is perfect. Just to give the correct terminology, if $E[\Delta Y]$ is not zero, then the moments are sometimes called the *non-central moments*. If you are dealing with non-central moments, you cannot interpret them directly as a statistical quantity (as the variance) anymore.

Note   If you are dealing with non-central moments, you cannot interpret them directly as a statistical quantity (as the variance) anymore. If the average of $\Delta Y^{[i]}$ is zero, then the MSE is simply the variance of the dIstributions of our predictions. And of course, the smaller the value, the better the predictions are.

Cross-Entropy

There are several ways to understand the cross-entropy loss function, but I think the most fascinating way is obtained by starting the discussion from information theory. In this section, we will discuss some of the fundamental concepts on a more intuitive basis to give you enough information and understanding to get a very powerful understanding of cross-entropy.

Self-Information or Suprisal of an Event

We need to start with the concept of self-information, or suprisal of an event. To get an intuitive understanding of it, consider the following: when an unlikely outcome of an event occurs, we associate it with a high level of information. When an outcome happens all the time, typically it does not have much information associated with it. In other words, we are more surprised when an unlikely event occurs; therefore, it's also called suprisal of an outcome. How can we formulate this in a mathematical form? Let's consider a random variable X with n possible outcomes $x_1, x_2, ..., x_n$ and probability mass function[7] $P(X)$. Let's indicate the probability of event x_i to occur with $p_i = P(x_i)$. Any monotonically decreasing function $I(p_i)$ between 0 and 1 could be used to represent the suprisal (or self-information) of the random variable X. But there is an important property that this function must have: if the events are independent, I should satisfy

$$I\left(p_i p_j\right) = I\left(p_i\right) + I\left(p_j\right)$$

If the outcomes i and j are independent. There is immediately a function that comes to mind that has this property: the logarithm. In fact, it's true that

$$\ln\left(p_i p_j\right) = \log p_i + \log p_j$$

To have it monotonically decreasing, we can choose the following formula:

$$I\left(p_i\right) = -\log p_i$$

---

[7]In probability and statistics, a probability mass function (PMF) is a function that gives the probability that a discrete random variable is exactly equal to some value [Stewart, William J. (2011). *Probability, Markov Chains, Queues, and Simulation: The Mathematical Basis of Performance Modeling*. Princeton University Press. p. 105. ISBN 978-1-4008-3281-1.]

Suprisal Associated with an Event X

In general, how much information do we have related to a specific event X? This is measured by the expected value over all possible outcomes for X (we will indicate this set with P). Mathematically, we can write this as

$$H(X) = E_P[I(X)] = \sum_{i=1}^{n} P(x_i)I(x_i) = -\sum_{i=1}^{n} P(x_i)\log_b P(x_i)$$

$H(X)$ is called the *Shannon entropy*, and b is the basis of the algorithm and typically is chosen as 2, 10, or e.

Cross-Entropy

Now let's suppose we want to compare two distributions of probabilities for our event X. Let's analyze what we do when we train a neural network for classification. Consider the following points:

- Our examples give us the "real" or expected distributions of our events (the true labels). Their distributions will be our P. For example, our observations may contain cat classes (let's suppose this is class 1) with a certain probability $P(x_1)$, where x_1 is the outcome "this image has a cat in it". We have a given probability mass function, P.

- The network we have trained will give us a different probability mass function, Q, since the predictions will not be identical to the training data. Outcome x_1 ("the image has a cat in it") will occur with a different probability, $Q(x_1)$. You will remember that when building a network for classification, we use a `softmax` activation function for the output layer to interpret the output as probabilities. Do you see how everything seems to make suddenly more sense?

We want to have a prediction that reflects as best as possible the given labels, meaning that we want to have a probability mass function Q that is as similar as possible to P.

To compare the two probability mass functions (what we are interested in), we can simply calculate the expected value of the self-information obtained by our network with the distribution obtained by the examples. In a more mathematical form

$$H(Q,P) = E_P\left[I(Q)\right] = E_P\left[-\log_b Q\right] = -\sum_{i=1}^{n} P(x_i)\log_b Q(x_i)$$

If you have any experience in information theory, $H(Q, P)$ will give a measure of the similary of the two probability mass functions, Q and P. To understand why, let's consider a practical example. X will be the toss of a fair coin. X will have two possible outcomes: x_1 will be the head and x_2 will be the tail of the coint. The "true" probability mass function is of course a constant one with $P(x_1) = 0.5$ and $P(x_2) = 0.5$. Now let's consider alternative probability mass functions Q_i with (we will consider only nine possible values for illustrative purposes):

- $i = 1 \rightarrow Q_1(x_1) = 0.1$, $Q_1(x_2) = 0.9$
- $i = 2 \rightarrow Q_2(x_1) = 0.2$, $Q_2(x_2) = 0.8$
- $i = 3 \rightarrow Q_3(x_1) = 0.3$, $Q_3(x_2) = 0.7$
- $i = 4 \rightarrow Q_4(x_1) = 0.4$, $Q_4(x_2) = 0.6$
- $i = 5 \rightarrow Q_5(x_1) = 0.5$, $Q_5(x_2) = 0.5$
- $i = 6 \rightarrow Q_6(x_1) = 0.6$, $Q_6(x_2) = 0.4$
- $i = 7 \rightarrow Q_7(x_1) = 0.7$, $Q_7(x_2) = 0.3$
- $i = 8 \rightarrow Q_8(x_1) = 0.8$, $Q_8(x_2) = 0.2$
- $i = 9 \rightarrow Q_9(x_1) = 0.9$, $Q_9(x_2) = 0.1$

Let's calculate $H(Q_i, P)$ for $i = 1, \ldots 5$. We don't need to calculate H for $i = 6, \ldots, 9$ since the function is symmetric, meaning for example that $H(Q_4, P) = H(Q_6, P)$. In Figure 5-1, you can see the plot of $H(Q_i, P)$. You can see how the maxium is reached for $i = 5$, exactly when the two probability mass functions are the same.

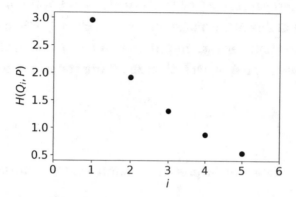

Figure 5-1. $H(Q_i, P)$ for $i = 1, \ldots 5$. The minimum is obtained for $i = 5$, when the two probability mass functions are exactly the same.

Note   Cross-entropy $H(Q, P)$ is a measure of how similar the two mass probability functions, Q and P, are.

Cross-Entropy for Binary Classification

Now let's consider a binary classification problem and let's see how cross-entropy works. Let's suppose our event X is the classification of a given image in two classes. The possible outcomes are only two: class 1 or class 2. Let's suppose for illustrative purposes that our image belongs to class 1. Our "true" probability mass function for the image will have $P(x_1) = 1.0$, $P(x_2) = 0$. In other words, our probability mass function P can only be 0 or 1 since we know the true value.

You will remember that in a binary classification problem we used the following

$$\mathcal{L}\left(\hat{y}^{(j)},y^{(j)}\right)=-\left(y^{(j)}\log\hat{y}^{(j)}+\left(1-y^{(j)}\right)\log\left(1-\hat{y}^{(j)}\right)\right)$$

Where $y^{(j)}$ represents the true labels (0 for class 1 and 1 for class 2) and $\hat{y}^{(j)}$ is the probability of the image j of being of class 2, or in other words, of the output of the network assuming the value 1. The cost function we will minimize is given by a sum over all observations (or examples)

$$J(w,b)=\frac{1}{m}\sum_{j=1}^{m}\mathcal{L}\left(\hat{y}^{(j)},y^{(j)}\right)$$

Using the notation of the previous section, we can write for image j

$$p_j\left(x_1\right)=1-y^{(j)}$$

$$p_j\left(x_2\right)=y^{(j)}$$

Remember that $y^{(j)}$ can be only 0 or 1; therefore, we have only two possibilities: $p_j(x_1) = 1$, $p_j(x_2) = 0$ or $p_j(x_1) = 0$, $p_j(x_2) = 1$. And we can also write for the prediction of the network

$$q_j\left(x_1\right)=1-\hat{y}^{(j)}$$

$$q_j\left(x_2\right)=\hat{y}^{(j)}$$

Remember: This result is determined by how we built our network (since we used the softmax activation functions in the output layer to have probabilities) and by how we coded our labels (to be 0 and 1, so that they could be interpreted as probabilities). Let's now write cross-entropy as defined in the previous section using our neural network notation but summing over all examples (remember that we want to have the entire cross-entropy for all the events, in other words for all images):

$$H(Q,P) = -\sum_{j=1}^{m}\sum_{i=1}^{2} p_j(x_i) \log_b q_j(x_i)$$

$$= -\sum_{j=1}^{m}\left(y^{(j)}\log_b \hat{y}^{(j)} + \left(1-y^{(j)}\right)\log_b\left(1-\hat{y}^{(j)}\right)\right)$$

So basically $\mathcal{L}\left(\hat{y}^{(i)},y^{(i)}\right)$ is nothing more than the cross-entropy as it is derived in information theory.

Note   Intuitively when we minimize the cross-entropy in a binary classification problem, we minimize the surprise that we may have when our predictions are different from what we expect.

$H(Q, P)$ measures how good our predictions probability mass function (Q) matches our training examples probability mass function (P).

Note   When we design a network for classification using the cross-entropy and we use the `softmax` activation function in the final layer to interpret the output as probabilities, we simply build a complex classification system that is based on information theory. We should thank Shannon[8] for classification with neural networks.

---

[8]https://en.wikipedia.org/wiki/Claude_Shannon

Cost Functions: A Final Word

It should be clear now that the cost function determines what a neural network can learn. Change it and the network will learn completely different things. It should come as no surprise that, to achieve special results, like art for example, it's simply a matter of choosing the right architecture and the right cost function. In the next part of this chapter, we will look at neural style transfer and it will become immediately clear how choosing the right cost function (multiple ones in this example as we will see) is the key to achieving extraordinary results.

Neural Style Transfer

At this point you have all the tools to start using networks for more advanced techniques: using pre-trained CNNs, extracting information from the hidden layers, and using custom cost functions. This is starting to be advanced material, so you need to understand all the basics we discussed in the previous chapters very well. If something seems unclear, go back and study the material again.

An interesting and fun application of CNNs is to make art. Neural style transfer (NST) refers to a technique that manipulates digital images, to adopt the appearance or style of another image[9]. A fun application is to take an image and let the network manipulate it to adopt it to the style of a famous painter, like Van Gogh. NST using deep learning appeared first in a paper by Gatys et al. in 2015[10]. It's a new technique. The method developed by Gatys used pre-trained deep CNNs to separate the content of an image from the style.

---

[9]https://en.wikipedia.org/wiki/Neural_Style_Transfer
[10]Gatys, Leon A.; Ecker, Alexander S.; Bethge, Matthias (26 August 2015). "A Neural Algorithm of Artistic Style". https://arxiv.org/abs/1508.06576

The idea is that an image is fed into a pre-trained VGG-19[11] CNN trained on the imagenet dataset. The author assumed that the content of an image can be found in the network intermediate layers output (the image passed through the learned filters in each layers), while the style lies in the correlations of the different layers output (coded in a Gramian matrix). The pre-trained network can identify the content of images quite well, and therefore the features learned by each layer must relate strongly to the content of the image, and not to the style. In fact, a robust CNN that is good at identifying images does not care much about style. Intuitively, style is contained in how the different filter responses over the space of an image are related. A painter may use brush strokes that are wide or narrow, may use many colors close to each other or just a few, and so on. Remember in a CNN, each layer is simply a collection of image filters; therefore, the output of a given layer is simply a collection of differently filtered versions of the input image10.

Another way of seeing that is that content is found when you look at an image from afar (you don't care much about the details), while style is found when looking at the image at a much closer scale and depends on how different parts of the image relate to each other. Gatys et al. have, in a smart way, simply implemented these ideas mathematically. To give you an idea, look at Figure 5-2. A network has manipulated the original image (upper left) into the style of the Van Gogh painting in the upper right, to obtain the image on the bottom.

---

[11]"Very Deep CNNS for Large-Scale Visual Recognition". Robots.ox.ac.uk. 2014. Retrieved 13 February 2019, http://www.robots.ox.ac.uk/~vgg/research/very_deep/

ORIGINAL IMAGE   STYLE IMAGE

MANIPULATED IMAGE

Figure 5-2. *An example of NST. The method has manipulated the original image (upper left) into the style of the Van Gogh painting in the upper right, to obtain the image on the bottom.*

The Mathematics Behind NST

The original paper used the VGG19 network, which Keras makes available for us to download and use. An input image that we will indicate here with x (I will try to use the original notation as much as possible) is encoded in each layer of the CNN. A layer with N_l filters (or kernels as they are sometimes called) will have N_l feature maps as output. In the algorithm those outputs will be flattened out in a one-dimensional vector of dimension M_l, where M_l is the height times the width of the output of each filter when applied to the input image. The response of a layer l can then be encoded in a tensor $F^l \in \mathbb{R}^{N_l \times M_l}$. Let's pause a second here and try to understand with a concrete example what we mean.

Let's suppose we use as input images in color, each with dimensions 32×32. Let's consider the first convolutional layer in a CNN that has been created with the code:

```
Conv2D(32, (3, 3), padding='same', activation='relu', input_
shape=input_shape))
```

Where of course `input_shape` = `(32,32,3)`. The output of the layer will have these dimensions

```
(None, 32, 32, 32)
```

Where of course the None will assume the value of the number of observations used. This is because we used the parameter `padding` = `'same'`. In this case, the output of layer $l = 1$, are 32 feature maps (or the result of the input image convoluted with the 32 filters) each with dimensions 32×32. In this case, we will have $N_{l=1} = 32$ and $M_{l=1} = 32 \times 32 = 1024$. Each of the 32×32 feature maps will be flattened out before calculating the Gramian matrices. You will see clearly how this is done later in the code.

Let's call the original image p. This is the image we want to change. The image that is generated as output is called x. We will indicate with P^l and F^l their respective features maps obtained from layer l. We define the squre error loss, called the *content loss function*, as follows:

$$\mathcal{L}_{content}(p,x,l) = \frac{1}{2}\sum_{i,j}\left(F_{ij}^l - P_{ij}^l\right)^2$$

In Keras, we will implement this with the following code:

```
content_loss = tf.add_n([tf.reduce_mean((content_outputs[name]-
content_targets[name])**2)
                            for name in content_outputs.
                            keys()])
```

where the `content_outputs[]` and `content_targets[]` will contain the output of specific layers of VGG19 when applied to the input (`content_outputs`) and the generated image (`content_targets`), respectively (already flattened). Later we will discuss it in more detail; don't worry for the moment if you don't understand it completely. You may wonder why we don't have the factor 1/2 but we don't need it, since $\mathcal{L}_{content}(p,x,l)$ will be multiplied by another factor, which will make the 1/2 useless.

We need to calculate the gradient of the loss function with respect to the image. This is quite an important point. What this means is that the parameters we want to learn are the pixel values of the image we want to change. The parameters of the network are fixed, and we don't need to change them. With Keras, we will need to use the `tape.gradient` function in this form:

```
tape.gradient(loss, image)
```

We will need to define the image as a TensorFlow `Variable` (more on that later). If you are not familiar with how `tape.gradient` works, I suggest you check out the official documentation at `https://www.tensorflow.org/tutorials/eager/automatic_differentiation`.

Note   The parameters we want to learn are the pixel values of the image we want to change, not the weights of the network.

Now we need to take care of the style. To do this, we need to define a loss function for the style. To do this, we need to define the Gramian matrix

G^l, which is the inner product between the flattened feature maps i and j in layer l. In other words

$$G^l_{ij} = \sum_k F^l_{ik} F^l_{kj}$$

With this newly defined quantity, we will define a Style loss function $\mathcal{L}_{style}(a,x)$, where a is the image from which we want to use the style as

$$\mathcal{L}_{style}(a,x) = \sum_{l=1}^{5} w_l E_l$$

Where

$$E_l = \frac{1}{4 N_l^2 M_l^2} \sum_{i,j} \left(G^l_{ij} - A^l_{ij} \right)^2$$

Where w_l are weights that in the original papers were chosen and equal 1/5. In Keras, we will implement this loss with the code (we will look at the details later):

```
tf.add_n([tf.reduce_mean((style_outputs[name]-style_
targets[name])**2)
                    for name in style_outputs.keys()])
```

The style_outputs and style_targets variables will contain the output of five of the layers of the VGG19 network. In the original paper, the following five layers were used:

```
l=1 - block1_conv1
l=2 - block2_conv1
l=3 - block3_conv1
l=4 - block4_conv1
l=5 - block5_conv1
```

Those are the first layers in each block in the VGG19 network. Remember that you can get the layer names from the VGG19 simply with this code:

```
vgg = tf.keras.applications.VGG19(include_top=False,
weights='imagenet')

print()
for layer in vgg.layers:
  print(layer.name)
```

That would give you this result:

```
input_1
block1_conv1
block1_conv2
block1_pool
block2_conv1
block2_conv2
block2_pool
block3_conv1
block3_conv2
block3_conv3
block3_conv4
block3_pool
block4_conv1
block4_conv2
block4_conv3
block4_conv4
block4_pool
block5_conv1
block5_conv2
block5_conv3
```

```
block5_conv4
block5_pool
```

Note that we have no dense layers, since we used `include_top=False`. Finally, we will minimize the following loss function

$$\mathcal{L}_{total}(p,x,a)=\alpha\mathcal{L}_{style}(a,x)+\beta\sum_{l=1}^{5}\mathcal{L}_{content}(p,x,l)$$

With gradient descent (for example), with respect to the image we want to change. The constants α and β can be choosen to give more weight to style or content. For the result in Figure 5-1, I chose $\alpha = 1.0$, $\beta = 10^4$. Other typical values are $\alpha = 10^{-2}$, $\beta = 10^4$.

An Example of Style Transfer in Keras

The code that we will discuss here has been taken from the original TensorFlow NST tutorial and is greatly simplified for this discussion. We will discuss only part of the code to simplify the discussion, since in its entirety the code is relatively long. You can find the entire simplified version in the book's GitHub repository in the Chapter 5 folder. I suggest you run the code in Google Colab with GPU enabled, since it is computationally quite intensive. To give you an idea, one epoch on my laptop takes roughly 13 seconds, while on Google Colab, it takes 0.5 seconds to work with 512×512 pixel images.

To make sure that you have the latest TensorFlow version installed, you should run the following code at the beginning of your notebook:

```
from __future__ import absolute_import, division, print_
function, unicode_literals
!pip install tensorflow-gpu==2.0.0-alpha0
import tensorflow as tf
```

If you run the code on Google Colab, you need to save the images you want to work with on your Google drive and mount it. To do that, you need to upload two images on your drive:

- A style image: For example, a famous painting. This is the image you want to get the style from.

- A content image: For example, a landscape or a photo you took. This is the image you want to modify.

I assume here that you uploaded your images into a folder called data into the root directory of your Google drive. What you need to do now is to mount your Google drive in Google Colab to be able to access the images. To do that, you need the following code:

```
from google.colab import drive
drive.mount('/content/drive')
```

If you run this code, you need to go to a specific URL (that will be given to you by Google Colab) where you will receive the code that you need to paste in your notebook. A nice overview on how to do this can be found at http://toe.lt/a. Once mounted, you'll get a list of the files in the directory with this:

```
!ls "/content/drive/My Drive/data"
```

We can define the filenames of the images we will use with

```
content_path = '/content/drive/My Drive/data/landscape.jpg'
style_path = '/content/drive/My Drive/data/vangogh_landscape.jpg'
```

You need to change the filenames to yours, of course. But you will find the images I used for this example on the GitHub repository if you want to try the exercise with them. You need to create the data directory if you don't have it and copy the images in there. The images will be loaded with the load_img() function. Note that in the function at the beginning we resize the images to have their maximum dimension equal

to 512 (the complete code for the load_img() function can be found on
GitHub). This is a size that is manageable, but if you want to generate
better-looking images, you need to increase this value. The image in
Figure 5-1 was generated with max_dim = 1024. The function begins with

```
def load_img(path_to_img):
  max_dim = 512
  img = tf.io.read_file(path_to_img)
```

So, you change the value of the max_dim variable to work with bigger
images. Now we need to select only the output of some layers, as we
described in the previous section. To do that, we put the names of the
layers we want to use into two lists:

```
# Content layer where will pull our feature maps
content_layers = ['block5_conv2']

# Style layer we are interested in
style_layers = ['block1_conv1',
                'block2_conv1',
                'block3_conv1',
                'block4_conv1',
                'block5_conv1']
```

This way we can select the right layers using the names. What we need
is a model that gets input and returns all the feature maps from each layer.
To do that, we use the following code

```
def vgg_layers(layer_names):
  vgg = tf.keras.applications.VGG19(include_top=False,
  weights='imagenet')
  vgg.trainable = False

  outputs = [vgg.get_layer(name).output for name in layer_names]
```

```
model = tf.keras.Model([vgg.input], outputs)
return model
```

This function gets a list as input with the layer names and selects the network layer output of the given layers with this line:

```
outputs = [vgg.get_layer(name).output for name in layer_names]
```

Note that there are no checks, so if you have a wrong layer names you will not get the result you expect. But since the layers we need are fixed, you don't need to check if the names exist in the network. This line

```
model = tf.keras.Model([vgg.input], outputs)
```

creates a model with one input (vgg.input) and one or more outputs, depending on the number of layers in the layer_names input list.

To calculate G_{ij}^l (the Gramian matrix), we use this function

```
def gram_matrix(input_tensor):
    result = tf.linalg.einsum('bijc,bijd->bcd', input_tensor,
    input_tensor)
    input_shape = tf.shape(input_tensor)
    num_locations = tf.cast(input_shape[1]*input_shape[2],
    tf.float32)
    return result/(num_locations)
```

where the variable num_locations is simply M_l. Now comes the interesting part: the definition of the loss functions. We need to define a class called StyleContentModel that will take our model and return the output of the different layers at each iteration. The class has an __init__ part that we will skip here (you can find the code in the Jupyter Notebook). The interesting part is the call() function:

```
def call(self, inputs):
    inputs = inputs*255.0
```

```
preprocessed_input = tf.keras.applications.vgg19.
preprocess_input(inputs)
outputs = self.vgg(preprocessed_input)
style_outputs, content_outputs = (outputs[:self.num_style_
layers],

                                   outputs[self.num_style_
                                   layers:])

style_outputs = [gram_matrix(style_output)
                 for style_output in style_outputs]

content_dict = {content_name:value
                for content_name, value
                in zip(self.content_layers, content_
                outputs)}

style_dict = {style_name:value
              for style_name, value
              in zip(self.style_layers, style_outputs)}

return {'content':content_dict, 'style':style_dict}
```

This function will return a dictionary with two elements—content_dict contains the content layers and their output and style_dict contains the style layers and their outputs. You use this function:

```
extractor = StyleContentModel(style_layers, content_layers)
```

And then:

```
style_targets = extractor(style_image)['style']
content_targets = extractor(content_image)['content']
```

This way, we can get the output of the different layers when applied to different images. Remember we need the output of the style layers when applied to our Van Gogh painting, but we need the content layer output when applied to the landscape (or your image) image. Let's save the content image (the landscape or your image) in a variable and define a function (it will be useful later9) that will clip the values of an array between 0 and 1:

```
image = tf.Variable(content_image)
def clip_0_1(image):
  return tf.clip_by_value(image, clip_value_min=0.0,
  clip_value_max=1.0)
```

Then we can define the two variables α, β as follows:

```
style_weight=1e-2
content_weight=1e4
```

Now we have everything we need to define the loss function:

```
def style_content_loss(outputs):
    style_outputs = outputs['style']
    content_outputs = outputs['content']
    style_loss = tf.add_n([tf.reduce_mean((style_outputs[name]-
    style_targets[name])**2)
                          for name in style_outputs.keys()])
    style_loss *= style_weight / num_style_layers

    content_loss = tf.add_n([tf.reduce_mean((content_
    outputs[name]-content_targets[name])**2)
                            for name in content_outputs.
                            keys()])
    content_loss *= content_weight / num_content_layers
    loss = style_loss + content_loss
    return loss
```

This code is rather self-explanatory, as we have discussed its parts already. This function expects as input the dictionary that we obtain using the StyleContentModel class.

Now let's create the function that will update the weights:

```
@tf.function()
def train_step(image):
  with tf.GradientTape() as tape:
    outputs = extractor(image)
    loss = style_content_loss(outputs)

  grad = tape.gradient(loss, image)
  opt.apply_gradients([(grad, image)])
  image.assign(clip_0_1(image))
```

We use `tf.GradientTape` to update the image. Note that when you annotate a function with `@tf.function`, you can still call it like any other function. But it will be compiled into a graph, which means you get the benefits of faster execution, running on GPU or TPU, or exporting to SavedModel (see `https://www.tensorflow.org/alpha/guide/autograph`). Remember that the variable `extractor` has been obtained with this code:

```
extractor = StyleContentModel(style_layers, content_layers)
```

And is the dictionary with the output of the different layers.

Now this code is rather advanced and complicated to understand at the beginning, so take your time and read the pages with the Jupyter Notebook open at the same time, to be able to follow the code and the explanation. Don't be discouraged if at the beginning you don't understand everything. The line:

```
grad = tape.gradient(loss, image)
```

will calculate the gradients of the loss function with respect to the variable `image` that we have defined. Each update step can be done with a simple line of code:

```
train_step(image)
```

Now we can do the final loop easily:

```
epochs = 20
steps_per_epoch = 100

step = 0
for n in range(epochs):
  for m in range(steps_per_epoch):
    step += 1
    train_step(image)
    print(".", end=")
  display.clear_output(wait=True)
  imshow(image.read_value())
  plt.title("Train step: {}".format(step))
  plt.show()
```

While it's running, you will see the image change every epoch and you can witness how it is changing.

NST with Silhouettes

There is a fun application that you can do with NST, and that has to do with silhouettes[12]. A *silhouette* is an image of something represented as a solid shape of a single color. In Figure 5-3, you can see an example; if you are a fan of *Star Wars*, you know who it is (hint: Darth Vader[13]).

---

[12]This part of the chapter has been inspired by the Medium post https://
becominghuman.ai/creating-intricate-art-with-neural-style-transfer-
e5fee5f89481.

[13]https://en.wikipedia.org/wiki/Darth_Vader

Figure 5-3. *A silhouette of the Star Wars character Darth Vader*

You should search the Internet[14] for images that are similar to a mosaic or stained glass, like the one shown in Figure 5-4.

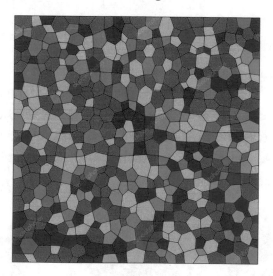

Figure 5-4. *A mosaic-like image*

---

[14]Note that all the images used in this chapter were images free of copyright and free to use. If you use images for your papers or block, ensure that you can use them freely or you'll need to pay royalties.

The goal is to obtain an image like the one shown in Figure 5-5.

Figure 5-5. *NST done on a silhouette after applying masking (more on this later)*

Masking

Masking has several meanings, depending on the field you are using it in. Here I refer to *masking* as the process of changing parts of an image to absolute white according to a silhouette. The idea is graphically illustrated in Figure 5-6. You can think of it this way: you put a silhouette over your image (they should have the same resolution) and keep only the parts where the silhouette is black.

Figure 5-6. *Masking applied to the mosaic image in Figure 5-4*

This is okay, but a bit unsatisfying, since for example you don't have edges in the result. The mosaic shapes are simply cut in the middle. Visually this is not so satisfying. But we can use NST to make the end image much nicer. The process is the following:

- You use the mosaic-like image as the style image.

- You use your silhouette image as the content image.

- At the end you apply masking to your end result using your silhouette image.

You can see the result (using the same code) in Figure 5-5. You can see that you get nice edges and the mosaic tiles are not cut in half.

You can find the entire code in the book's GitHub repository in Chapter 5. But as a reference, let's suppose that you have your image saved as a numpy array. Let's suppose that the silhouette is saved in an array called mask and that your image is saved in an array called result. The assumption (and you should check that) is that the mask array will contain only 0 or 255 values (black and white). Then masking is done simply with this:

```
result[mask] = 255
```

That simply makes white in the result image where there is white in the silhouette and leaves the rest untouched.

CHAPTER 6

Object Classification: An Introduction

In this chapter, we will look at more advanced tasks in image processing that can be achieved with neural networks. We will look at semantic segmentation, localization, detection, and instance segmentation. The goal of this chapter is not to make you an expert, since one could easily read many books on the subject, but to give you enough information to be able to understand the algorithms and read the original papers. I hope that, by the end of this chapter, you will understand the difference between the methods, and you will have an intuitive understanding of the building blocks of these methods.

These algorithms need many advanced techniques that we have looked at in the previous chapters, like multiple loss functions and multi-task learning. We will look at a few more in this chapter. Keep in mind that the original papers on the methods are in some cases just a couple of years old, so to master the subject, you need to get your hands dirty and read the original papers.

Training and using the networks described in the papers is not doable on a simple laptop and therefore you will find in this chapter (and in the next) less code and examples. I try to point you in the right direction and tell you what pre-trained libraries and networks are available at the time of this writing, in case you want to use those techniques in your own

© Umberto Michelucci 2019
U. Michelucci, *Advanced Applied Deep Learning*,
https://doi.org/10.1007/978-1-4842-4976-5_6

projects. That will be the subject of the next chapter. Where relevant, I try to point out the differences, advantages, and disadvantages of the different methods. We will look at the most advanced methods in a very superficial way, since the details are so complex that only studying the original papers can give you all the information you need to implement those algorithms yourself.

What Is Object Localization?

Let's start with an intuitive understanding of what object localization is. We have already seen image classification in many forms: it tells us what the content of an image is. That may sound easy, but there are many cases when this is difficult, and not because of the algorithms. For example, consider the case when you have a dog *and* a cat in an image at the same time. What is the class of the image: cat or dog? And what is the content of the image: A cat or a dog? Of course, both are in there, but classification algorithms give you one class only, so they are unable to tell you that you have two animals in the image. And what if you have many cats and many dogs? What if you have several objects? You get the idea.

It may be interesting to know where the cat and the dog are in the image. Consider the problem of a self-driving car: it is important to know where a person is, since that could mean the difference between a dead passerby and a living one. Classification, as we have looked at in the previous chapters, often cannot be used alone to solve real-life problems with images. Typically, recognizing that you have many instances of an object in an image involves finding their position in an image and being able to distinguish between them. To do that, we need to be able to find the positions of each instance in the image and their borders. This is one of the most interesting (and more difficult) tasks in image recognition techniques that can be solved with CNNs.

Typically, with object localization we want to determine the location of an object (for example, a person or a car) in an image and draw a rectangular bounding box around it.

Note   With object localization, we want to determine the location of one or more objects (for example, people or cars) in an image and draw a rectangular bounding box around it.

Sometimes in the literature researchers use the term *localization* when the image contains only one instance of an object (for example, only one person or only one car) and the term *detection* when an image contains several instances of an object.

Note   *Localization* typically refers to when an image contains only one instance of an object, while *detection* is when there are several instances of an object in an image.

To summarize and clarify the terminology, here is an overview of all the words and terms used (a visual explanation is shown in Figure 6-1):

- **Classification**: Give a label to an image, or in other words, "understand" what is in an image. For example, an image of a cat may have the label "cat" (we have seen several cases of this in the previous chapters).

- **Classification and localization**: Give a label to an image and determine the borders of the object contained in it (and typically draw a rectangle around the object).

- **Object detection**: This term is used when you have multiple instances of an object in an image. In object detection, you want to determine all the instances of several objects (for example, people, cars, signs, etc.) and draw bounding boxes around them.

- **Instance segmentation**: You want to label each pixel of the image with a specific class for each separate instance, to be able to find the exact limits of the object instance.

- **Semantic segmentation**: You want to label each pixel of the image with a specific class. The difference with instance segmentation is that you don't care if you have several instances of a car as examples. All pixels belonging to the cars will be labelled as "car". In instance segmentation, you will still be able to tell how many instances of a car you have and where they are exactly. To understand the difference, see Figure 6-1.

Figure 6-1. *A visual explanation of the different terms describing the general task of locating one or more objects in an image*

Segmentation is typically the most difficult task of all of them, and in particular instance segmentation is particularly difficult. Many advanced techniques come together to solve those problems. One of the things to remember is that getting enough training data is not easy. Keep in mind that this is much more difficult than simple classification, since someone will need to mark where the objects are. With segmentation, someone needs to classify each pixel in the image, which means training data is very expensive and difficult to collect.

Most Important Available Datasets

A well-known dataset that can be used to work on these problems is the Microsoft COCO dataset at `http://cocodataset.org`. The dataset contains 91 object types with a total of 2.5 million labelled instances in 328,000 images.[1] To give you an idea of the kind of labeling used, Figure 6-2 shows some examples from the dataset. You can see how specific instances of objects (like people and cats) are classified at the pixel level.

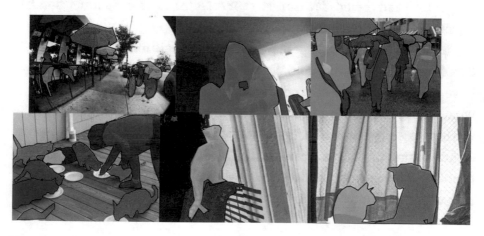

Figure 6-2. *Examples of the images in the COCO dataset*

---

[1]The original paper describing the dataset is: Tsung-Yi Lin, Michael Maire, Serge Belongie, Lubomir Bourdev, Ross Girshick, James Hays, Pietro Perona, Deva Ramanan, C. Lawrence Zitnick, Piotr Dollár, *Microsoft COCO: Common Objects in Context,* `https://arxiv.org/abs/1405.0312`

A quick note about sizes: the 2017 training images are roughly 118,000 and require 18GB[2] of hard disk space, so keep that in mind. Training a network with such a large amount of data is not trivial and will require time and lots of computing power. There is an API to download the COCO images that you can use and that is also available in Python. More information can be found on the main web page or on the API GitHub repository at `https://github.com/cocodataset/cocoapi`. The images have five annotation types: object detection, keypoint detection, stuff segmentation, panoptic segmentation, and image captioning. More information can be found at `http://cocodataset.org/#format-data`.

Another dataset that you may encounter is the Pascal VOC dataset. Unfortunately, the website is not that stable, and therefore mirrors exist where you can find the files. One mirror is `https://pjreddie.com/projects/pascal-voc-dataset-mirror/`. Note that this is a much smaller dataset than the COCO dataset.

In this and the next chapter, we will concentrate mainly on object classification and localization. We will assume that in the images we have only one instance of a specific object, and the task is to determine what kind of object it is and draw a bounding box (a rectangle) around it. These present enough challenge for now! We will look briefly at how segmentation works, but we will not go into many details about it, since its problems are extremely difficult to solve. I will provide references that you may check and study on your own.

Intersect Over Union (IoU)

Let's consider the task of classifying an image and then drawing a bounding box around the object in it. In Figure 6-3, you can see an example of the output we expect (where the class would be cat).

Figure 6-3. *An example of object classification and localization*[3]

This is a fully supervised task. This means that we will need to learn where the bounding boxes are and compare them to some given ground truth. We need a metric to quantify how good the overlap is between the predicted bounding boxes and the ground truth. This is typically done with the IOU (Intersect Over Union) . In Figure 6-4, you can see a visual explanation of it. As a formula, we could write

$$IOU = \frac{Area\ of\ overlap}{Area\ of\ union}$$

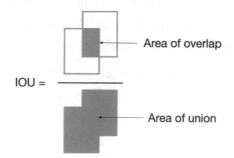

Figure 6-4. *A visual explanation of the IOU metric*

---

[3]Image source: http://www.cbsr.ia.ac.cn/users/ynyu/detection.html

In the ideal case of perfect overlap, we have $IOU = 1$, while if there is no overlap at all, we have $IOU = 0$. You will find this term in blogs and books, so it's a good idea to know how to measure bounding boxes using the ground truth.

A Naïve Approach to Solving Object Localization (Sliding Window Approach)

A naïve way of solving the problem of localization is the following (spoiler: this is a bad idea but it's instructive to see why):

1. You cut a small portion of your input image starting from the top-left corner. Let's suppose your image has dimensions x, y, and your portion has dimensions w_x, w_y, with $w_x < x$ and $w_y < y$.

2. You use a pre-trained network (how you train it or how you get it is not relevant here) and you let it classify the image portion that you cut.

3. You shift this window by an amount we call *stride* and indicate with s toward the right and then below. You use the network to classify this second portion.

4. Once the sliding window has covered the entire image, you choose the position of the window that gives you the highest classification probability. This position will give you the bounding box of your object (remember your window has dimensions w_x, w_y).

In Figure 6-5, you can see a graphical illustration of the algorithm (we assumed $w_x = w_y = s$).

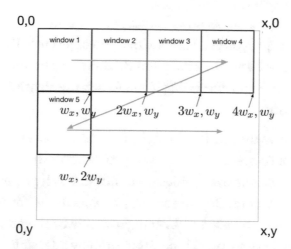

Figure 6-5. *A graphical illustration of the sliding window approach to solve the problem of object localization*

As you can see in Figure 6-5, we start from the top left and slide the window toward the right. As soon as we reach the right border of the image and we don't have any space to shift the window further to the right, we get back on the left border but we shift it s pixel down. We continue in this fashion until we reach the lower-right corner of the image.

You might immediately see some problems with this method:

- Depending on the choice of w_x, w_y, and s, we may not be able to cover the entire image. (Do you see in Figure 6-5 the small portion of the image on the right of window 4 that remains not analyzed?)

- How do you choose w_x, w_y, and s? This is a rather nasty problem, since the bounding box of our object will have exactly the dimensions w_x, w_y. What if the object is larger or smaller? We typically don't know in advance its dimensions and that is a huge problem if we want to have precise bounding boxes.

- What if our object flows across two windows? In Figure 6-5, you can imagine that the object is half in window 2 and half in window 3. Then your bounding box would not be correct if you follow the algorithm as described.

We could solve the third problem by using $s = 1$ to be sure that we cover all possible cases, but the first two problems are not so easy to solve. To address the window size problem, we should try all possible sizes and all possible proportions. Do you see any problem here? The number of evulations that you will need to do with your network is getting out of control and will become quickly computationally infeasible.

Problems and Limitations the with Sliding Window Approach

In the book's GitHub repository, within the Chapter 6 folder, you can find an implementation of the sliding window algorithm. To make things easier, I decided to use the MNIST dataset since you should know it very well at this point and it's an easy dataset to use. As a first step, I built a CNN trained on the MNIST dataset that reached 99.3% accuracy. I then proceeded to save the model and the weights on disk. The CNN I used has the following structure:

Layer (type)	Output Shape	Param #
===	===	===
conv2d_1 (Conv2D)	(None, 26, 26, 32)	320
conv2d_2 (Conv2D)	(None, 24, 24, 64)	18496
max_pooling2d_1 (MaxPooling2	(None, 12, 12, 64)	0
dropout_1 (Dropout)	(None, 12, 12, 64)	0
flatten_1 (Flatten)	(None, 9216)	0
dense_1 (Dense)	(None, 128)	1179776
dropout_2 (Dropout)	(None, 128)	0
dense_2 (Dense)	(None, 10)	1290

Total params: 1,199,882
Trainable params: 1,199,882
Non-trainable params: 0

I then saved the model and weights using this code (we already discussed how to do this):

```
model_json = model.to_json()
with open("model_mnist.json", "w") as json_file:
    json_file.write(model_json)
model.save_weights("model_mnist.h5")
```

You can see in Figure 6-6 how the network training and accuracy changes with the number of epochs.

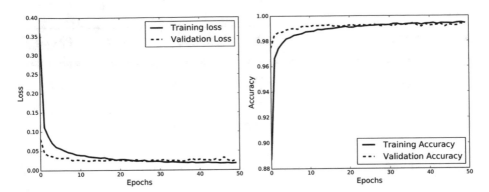

Figure 6-6. *Loss function value and accuracy for the training (continuous line) and for the validation (dashed line) dataset versus the number of epochs*

The weights and model can be found in the GitHub repository. I did that to avoid having to re-train the CNN every time. I can reuse the model every time by reloading it. You can do it with this code (after you mount your Google drive if you want to run the code in Google Colab as I did):

```
model_path = '/content/drive/My Drive/pretrained-models/model_
mnist.json'
weights_path = '/content/drive/My Drive/pretrained-models/
model_mnist.h5'

json_file = open(model_path, 'r')
loaded_model_json = json_file.read()
json_file.close()
loaded_model = model_from_json(loaded_model_json)
loaded_model.load_weights(weights_path)
```

To make things easier. I decided to create a larger image with one digit in the middle and see how efficiently I can put a bounding box around it. To create the image, I used the following code:

```
from PIL import Image, ImageOps
src_img = Image.fromarray(x_test[5].reshape(28,28))
newimg = ImageOps.expand(src_img,border=56,fill='black')
```

The resulting image is 140x140 pixel. You can see it in Figure 6-7.

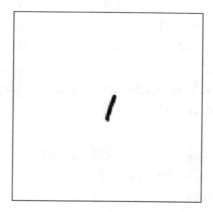

Figure 6-7. *The new image created by adding a white border of 56 pixels around one of the digits in the MNIST dataset*

Now let's start with a sliding window that's 28x28 pixels. We can write a function that will try to localize the digit and that will get the image as input, the stride *s*, and the values w_x and w_y:

```
def localize_digit(bigimg, stride, wx, wy):
  slidx, slidy = wx, wy

  digit_found = -1
  max_prob = -1
  bbx = -1 # Bounding box x upper left
  bby = -1 # Bounding box y upper left
  max_prob_ = 0.0
  bbx_ = -1
  bby_ = -1
  most_prob_digit = -1
```

```
maxloopx = (bigimg.shape[0] -wx) // stride
maxloopy = (bigimg.shape[1] -wy) // stride
print((maxloopx, maxloopy))

for slicey in range (0, maxloopx*stride, stride):
  for slicex in range (0, maxloopy*stride, stride):
    slice_ = bigimg[slicex:slicex+wx, slicey:slicey+wx]
    img_ = Image. fromarray(slice_).resize((28, 28), Image.
    NEAREST)
    probs = loaded_model.predict(np.array(img_).
    reshape(1,28,28,1))
    if (np.max(probs > 0.2)):
      most_prob_digit = np.argmax(probs)
      max_prob_ = np.max(probs)
      bbx_ = slicex
      bby_ = slicey

    if (max_prob_ > max_prob):
      max_prob = max_prob_
      bbx = bbx_
      bby = bby_
      digit_found = most_prob_digit

print("Digit "+str(digit_found)+ " found, with probability
"+str(max_prob)+" at coordinates "+str(bbx)+" "+str(bby))

return (max_prob, bbx, bby, digit_found)
```

Running on our image as so:

```
localize_digit(np.array(newimg), 28, 28, 28)
```

Returns this code:

```
Digit 1 found, with probability 1.0 at coordinates 56 56
(1.0, 56, 56, 1)
```

The resulting bounding boxes can be seen in Figure 6-8.

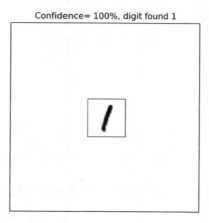

Figure 6-8. *The bounding box found by the sliding window method with $w_x = 28$, $w_y = 28$, and stride $s = 28$*

So that works quite well. But you may have noticed that we used values for w_x, w_y, and s that are exactly 28, which is the size of our images. What happens if we change that? For example, consider the cases depicted in Figure 6-9. You can clearly see how this method stops working as soon as the size and proportions of the window change to different values than 28.

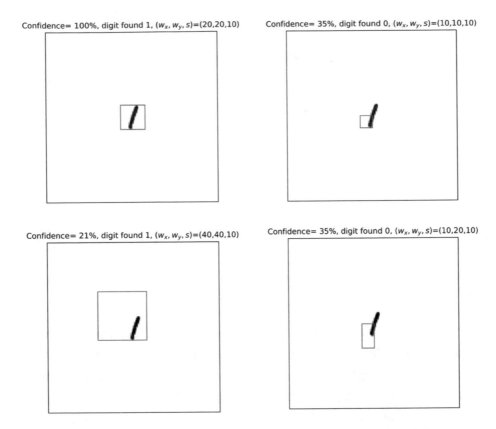

Figure 6-9. *Results of the sliding window algorithm with different values of* w_x, w_y, *and s*

Check the confidence of the classification in Figure 6-9, in the lower-left box. It is quite low. For example, for a window 40x40 and a stride of 10, the classification of the digit is correct (a 1) but is done with a probability of 21%. That's a low value! In the lower-right box, the classification is completely wrong. Keep in mind that you need to resize the small portion you cut from your image, and therefore it may look different from the training data you used.

In this case, it may seem easy to choose the right window size and proportions, since you know what the images looks like, but in general you have no idea what value will work. You would have to test different proportions and sizes and get several possible bounding boxes and classifications and then decide which one is the best. You can easily see how this becomes computationally infeasible with real images that may contain several objects with different dimensions and proportions.

Classification and Localization

We have seen that the sliding window approach is a bad idea. A better approach is to use multi-task learning. The idea is that we can build a network that will learn at the same time the class and the position of the bounding box. We can achieve that by adding two dense layers after the last one of a CNN. One with (for example) N_c neurons (to classify N_c classes) that will predict the class with a cross-entropy loss function (that we will indicate with $J_{classification}$), and one with four neurons that will learn the bounding boxes with a ℓ_2 loss function (that we will indicate with J_{BB}). You can see a diagram of the network in Figure 6-10.

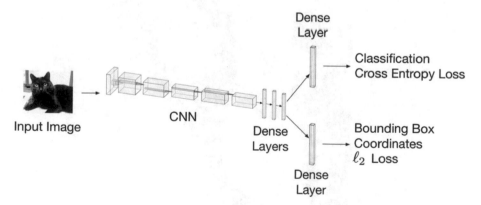

Figure 6-10. *A diagram that depicts a network that can predict the class and the bounding box position at the same time*

Since this will be a multi task learning problem, we will need to minimize a linear combination of the two loss functions:

$$J_{classification} + \alpha J_{BB}$$

Of course, α is an additional hyper-parameter that needs to be tuned. Just as a reference a ℓ_2 loss is proportional to the MSE

$$\ell_2 \; Loss \; Function = \sum_{i=1}^{m} \left(y_{true}^{(i)} - y_{predicted}^{(i)} \right)^2$$

Where we have, as usual, indicated with m the number of observations we have at our disposal. This same idea is used very successfully in human pose estimation, which finds specific points of the human body (like for example, the joints), as can be seen in Figure 6-11.

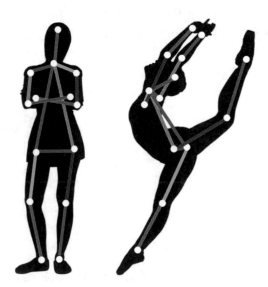

Figure 6-11. *An example of human pose estimation. A CNN can be trained to find important points of the human body, such as the joints.*

There is a lot of research going on in this field, and in the next sections we will look at how those methods work. The implementation becomes quite complex and time consuming. If you want to work with these algorithms, the best way is to look at the original papers and study them. Unfortunately, there is no plug-and-play library that you can use for those tasks, although you may find a GitHub repository that will help you. In this chapter, we will look at the most common variations of CNNs to do object localization—R-CNN, fast R-CNN, and faster R-CNN. In the next chapter, we will look at the YOLO (You Only Look Once) algorithm. The next sections should serve only as pointers to the relevant papers and will give you a basic understanding of the building blocks of the networks. This is by no means an exhaustive analysis of these implementations, as that would require a massive amount of space.

Region-Based CNN (R-CNN)

The basic idea of region-based CNNs (also known as R-CNNs) is quite simple (but implementing it is not). As we discussed, the main problem with naïve approaches is that you need to test a huge number of windows to be able to find the best matching bounding boxes. Searching every possible location is computationally infeasible, as it is testing all possible aspect ratios and window sizes.

So Girshick et al.[4] proposed a method where they used an algorithm called selective search[5] to first propose 2000 regions from the image (called the region proposals) and then, instead of classifying a huge number of regions, they classified just those 2000 regions.

---

[4] https://arxiv.org/pdf/1311.2524.pdf

[5] Jasper R. R. Uijlings, Koen E. A. van de Sande, Theo Gevers, Arnold W. M. Smeulders *International Journal of Computer Vision,* Volume 104 (2), page 154-171, 2013 [http://toe.lt/b]

Selective search has nothing to do with machine learning and uses a classical approach to determine which regions may contain an object. The first step in the algorithm is to segment an image, using pixel intensities and graph-based methods (for example, the one by Felzenszwalb and Huttenlocher[6]). You can see in Figure 6-12 the result of this segmentation.

Figure 6-12. *An example of segmentation applied to an image (image source:* `http://cs.brown.edu/people/pfelzens/segment/`*)*

After this step, adjacent regions are grouped together based on similarities of the following features:

- Color similarity

- Texture similarity

---

[6]P. Felzenszwalb, D. Huttenlocher, *Efficient Graph-Based Image Segmentation, International Journal of Computer Vision,* Vol. 59, No. 2, September 2004

- Size similarity

- Shape compatibility

The exact details of how this is done go beyond the scope of this book, since those techniques are typically used in image-processing algorithms.

In the OpenCV[7] library, there is an implementation of the algorithm that you can try. In Figure 6-13, you can see an example. I applied the algorithm to a picture I took and I asked the algorithm to propose 40 regions.

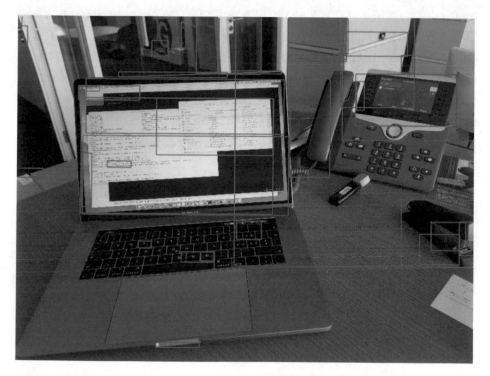

Figure 6-13.   *An example of the output of the selective search algorithm as implemented in the OpenCV library*

---

[7]https://opencv.org

The Python code that I used can be found on the following website: `https://www.learnopencv.com/selective-search-for-object-detection-cpp-python/`. The main idea of R-CNN is to use a CNN to label the regions that this algorithm proposed and then use support vector machines for the final classification.

In Figure 6-9, you can see for example that the laptop has not been identified as an object. But that is why one uses 2000 regions in R-CNN, to make sure that enough regions are proposed. Checking many regions manually cannot be done visually by a person. The number of regions and their overlap is so big that the task is not feasible anymore. If you try the OpenCV implementation of the algorithm, you will notice that it is quite slow. This is one of the main reasons that additional methods have been developed. The manual approach is, for example, not suitable for real-time object detection (for example, in a self driving car).

R-CNN can be summarized in the following steps (the steps have been taken from `http://toe.lt/d`):

1. Take a pre-trained `imagenet` CNN (such as Alexnet).

2. Re-train the last fully connected layer with the objects that need to be detected and the "no-object" class.

3. Get all proposals (around 2000 region proposals for each image) from selective search and resize them to match the CNN input.

4. Train SVM to classify each region between object
    and background (one binary SVM for each class).

5. Use bounding box regression. Train a linear
    regression classifier that will output some correction
    factor for the bounding boxes.

Fast R-CNN

Girshick improved on its algorithm and created what are known as
"fast R-CNNs".[8] The main idea behind this algorithm is the following

1. The image goes through the CNN and feature maps
    are extracted (the output of the convolutional
    layers).

2. Regions are proposed, not based on the initial
    image, but based on the feature maps.

3. Then the same feature maps and the proposed
    regions are used passed to a classifier that decides
    which object is in which region.

A diagram explaining these steps is shown in Figure 6-14.

---

[8]https://arxiv.org/pdf/1504.08083.pdf

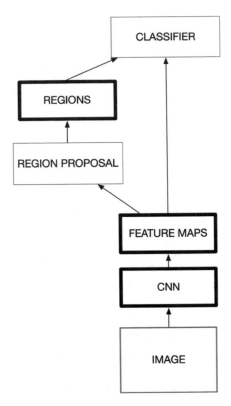

Figure 6-14. *A diagram depicting the main steps of the algorithm for fast R-CNN*

The reason this algorithm is faster than R-CNN is because you don't have to feed 2000 region proposals to the convolutional neural network every time[9]—you do it only once.

---

[9]http://toe.lt/c

Faster R-CNN

Note that R-CNN and fast R-CNN both use selective search to propose regions, and therefore are relatively slow. Even fast R-CNN needs around two seconds for each image, making this variation not suitable for real-time object detection. R-CNN needs around 50 seconds, and fast R-CNN around two seconds. But it turns out we can do even better, by removing the need to use selective search, since this turns out to be the bottleneck of both algorithms.

Ren et al.[10] developed a new idea: to use a neural network to learn regions from labelled data, removing the slow selective search algorithm altogether. Faster R-CNN requires around 0.2 seconds, making them a fast algorithm for object detection. There is a very nice diagram depicting the main steps of a faster R-CNN that can be found at `http://toe.lt/e`.[11] We report it in Figure 6-15 for you since I think it really helps in intuitively understanding the main building blocks of a faster R-CNN. The details tend to be quite complicated and therefore an intuitive and superficial description will not serve you. To understand the steps and the subtleties, you need more time and experience.

---

[10]`https://arxiv.org/pdf/1506.01497.pdf`

[11]Part of the image appears in the original paper by Ren, but additional labels and information have been added by Leonardo Araujo dos Santos (`https://legacy.gitbook.com/@leonardoaraujosantos`).

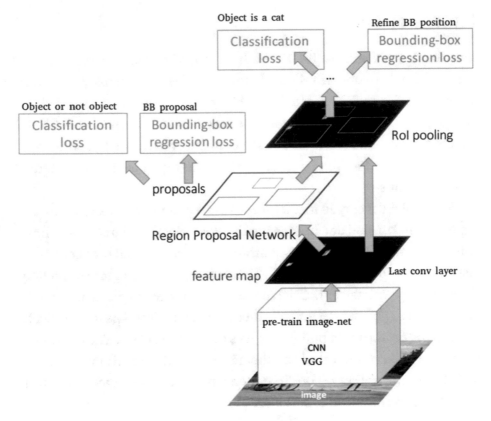

Figure 6-15. *A diagram depicting the main parts of faster R-CNN. Image source:* `http://toe.lt/e.`

In the next chapter, we will look at another algorithm (YOLO) and see how you can use those techniques in your own projects.

## CHAPTER 7

Object Localization: An Implementation in Python

In this chapter, we will look at the YOLO (You Only Look Once) method for object detection. The chapter is split in two parts: in the first section we learn how the algorithm works, and in the second section, I will give an example of how you can use it in your own Python projects.

Keep in mind that YOLO is quite complicated, so for 99% of you, a pre-trained model is the best choice for doing object detection. For the 1% at the forefront of the research, you probably don't need this book anyway and you should know how to do object detection starting from scratch.

This chapter (as the previous one) should serve to point you in the right direction, give you the fundamentals you need to understand the algorithm, and give you your first experiences with object detection. You will notice quite soon that those methods are slow, difficult to implement, and have many limitations. This is a very active research field that is also very young. The paper describing YOLO version 3 (that we will use later in the chapter in the Python code) was published just in April, 2018. At the time of this writing, it's less than two years old!

© Umberto Michelucci 2019
U. Michelucci, *Advanced Applied Deep Learning*,
https://doi.org/10.1007/978-1-4842-4976-5_7

Those algorithms are difficult to implement, difficult to understand, and very difficult to train. I hope that by the end of this chapter, you will understand the basics of it, and you can perform your first tests with the models.

Note   Those algorithms are difficult to implement, difficult to understand, and very difficult to train.

The You Only Look Once (YOLO) Method

In the last chapter, we looked at several methods for object detection. I also showed you why using a sliding window is a bad idea and where the difficulties are. In 2015, Redmon J. et al. proposed a new method to do object detection: they called it YOLO (You Only Look Once). They developed a network that can perform all the necessary tasks (detect where the objects are, classify multiple objects, etc.) in one pass. This is one of the reasons that this method is fast and is used often in real-time applications.

In the literature, you will find three versions of the algorithm: YOLOv1, YOLOv2, and YOLOv3. v2 and v3 are improvements over v1 (more on that later). The original network has been developed and trained with *darknet*, a neural network framework developed by the author of the original algorithm, Redmon J. You will not find an easy-to-download, pre-trained model that you can use with Keras. More on that later when I give you an example of how you can use it in your projects.

It is very instructive to read the original paper on YOLO, which can be found at https://arxiv.org/abs/1506.02640.

Note   The main idea of the method is to reframe the detection problem as one single regression problem, from the pixels of the image as inputs, to the bounding box coordinates and class probabilities[1].

Let's see how it works in detail.

How YOLO Works

To understand how YOLO works, it's best to go through the algorithm step by step.

Dividing the Image Into Cells

The first step is to divide the image into $S \times S$ cells. For each cell, we predict what (and if an) object is in the cell. Only one object will be predicted for each cell, so one cell cannot predict multiple objects. Then for each cell, a certain number (B) of bounding boxes that should contain the object are predicted. In Figure 7-1, you can see the grid and the bounding boxes that the network might predict (as an example). In the original paper, the image was divided into a 7 × 7 grid, but for the sake of clarity in Figure 7-1, I divided the image into a 5x5 grid.

---

[1]Redmon J. et al., "You Only Look Once: Unified, Real-Time Object Detection," https://arxiv.org/abs/1506.02640.

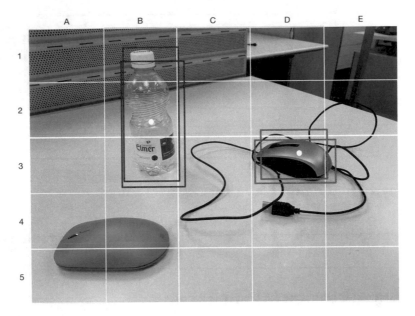

Figure 7-1. *Image divided into a 5 × 5 grid. For cell D3, we will predict the mouse and will predict bounding boxes (the yellow boxes). For cell B2, we will predict a bottle and its bounding boxes (the red rectangles).*

Let's take as an example cell D3 in Figure 7-1. This cell will predict the presence of a mouse and then it will predict a certain number *B* of bounding boxes (the yellow rectangles). Similarly, cell B2 will predict the presence of the bottle and *B* bounding boxes (the red rectangles in Figure 7-1) all at the same time. Additionally, the model predicts a class confidence (a number) for each bounding box. To be precise, the model output for each cell is as follows:

- For each bounding box (*B* in total), there are four values: *x*, *y*, *w*, *h*. These are the position of the center, its width, and its height. Note that the position of the center is given with relationship to the cell position, not as an absolute value.

- For each bounding box (B in total), there is a confidence score, which is a number that reflects how likely the box contains the object. In particular, at training time, if we indicate the probability of the cell containing the object as Pr($Object$), the confidence is calculated as follows:

$$Pr(Object) \times IOU$$

Where IOU indicates the Intersection Over Union, which is calculated using the training data (see the previous chapter for an explanation of the term and how to calculate it). This number encodes at the same time the probability that a specific object is in a box and how good the bounding box fits the object.

Therefore, supposing we have $S = 5$, $B = 2$ and supposing the network can classify $N_c = 80$ classes, the network will have an output of size of the following:

$$S \times S \times (B \times 5 + N_c) = 5 \times 5 \times (2 \times 5 + 80) = 2250$$

In the original paper, the authors used $S = 7$, $B = 2$ and used the VOC dataset[2] with 20 labelled classes. Therefore, the output of the network was as follows:

$$S \times S \times (B \times 5 + N_c) = 7 \times 7 \times (2 \times 5 + 20) = 1470$$

The network structure is quite easy. It's simply a set of several convolutional layers (with some maxpool thrown in there) and a big dense layer at the end to predict the necessary values (remember the problem is

---

[2]http://host.robots.ox.ac.uk/pascal/VOC/

framed as a regression problem). In the original paper, the authors were inspired by the GoogLeNet model. The network has 24 layers followed by two dense layers (the last one having 1470 neurons; do you see why?). Training took, as the authors mentioned, one entire week. They used a few tricks for the training, and if you are interested, I strongly suggest you read the original paper. It's quite instructive (for example, they also used learning rate decay in an unusual way, increasing the value of the learning rate at the beginning and then lowering it later). They also used dropout and extensive data augmentation. Training those models is not a trivial undertaking.

YOLOv2 (Also Known As YOLO9000)

The original YOLO version had some shortcomings. For example, it was not very good at detecting objects that were too close. In the second version,[3] the authors introduced some optimizations, the most important one being *anchor boxes*. The network gives pre-determined sets of boxes, and instead of predicting bounding boxes completely from scratch, it simply predicted deviations from the set of anchor boxes. The anchor boxes can be chosen depending on the type of objects that you want to predict, making the network better at certain specific tasks (for example, small or big objects).

In this version, they also changed the network structure, using 19 layers and then 11 more layers specifically designed for object detection, for a total of 30 layers. This version also struggled with small objects (also when using anchor boxes). This was because the layers downsampled the image and, during the forward pass-through, the network information was lost, making detecting small things difficult.

---

[3]Redmon J., Farhadi A., "YOLO9000: Better, Faster, Stronger," https://arxiv.org/abs/1612.08242

YOLOv3

The last version[4] introduces a few new concepts that makes the model quite powerful. Here are the main improvements:

- Predicting boxes at different scales: The model predicts boxes with different dimensions, so to say (is a bit more complicated than that, but that should give you an intuitive understanding of what is going on).

- The network is much bigger: A total of 53 layers.

- The network uses skip connections. Basically, this means that the output of a layer will be fed not only to the very next layer but also to a layer coming later in the network. This way, the information not yet downsampled will be used later to make detecting small objects easier. Skip connections are used in ResNets (not discussed in this book), and you can find a good introduction at http://toe.lt/w.

- This version uses nine anchor boxes, three for each scale.

- This version predicts more bounding boxes for each cell.

All those improvements make YOLOv3 quite good, but also quite slow, due to the increased computational power needed to process all those numbers.

---

[4]Redmon J., Farhadi A., "YOLOv3: An Incremental Improvement," https://arxiv.org/pdf/1804.02767.pdf

Non-Maxima Suppression

Once you have all the predicted bounding boxes, you need to choose the best one. Remember that for each cell and object, the model predicts several bounding boxes (regardless of which version you use). Basically, you choose the best bounding box by following this procedure (called *non-maxima suppression*):

1. It first discards all cells in which the probability of an object being present is less than a given threshold (typically 0.6).

2. It takes all the cells with the highest probability of having an object inside.

3. It takes the bounding boxes that have the highest score and removes all other bounding boxes that have an IOU greater than a certain threshold (typically 0.5) with each other. That means that it removes all bounding boxes that are very similar to the chosen one.

Loss Function

Note that the networks mentioned previously have a large number of outputs, so you should not expect a simple loss function to work. Also note that different parts of the final layer have very different meanings. One part is bounding box positions, one part is class probabilities, and so on. The loss function has three parts:

- Classification loss

- Localization loss (the error between predicted bounding boxes and the expected results)

- Confidence loss (whether there is an object in the box)

Let's take a closer look at these three aspects of loss.

Classification Loss

The classification loss used is determined by

$$\sum_{i=0}^{S^2} \mathbb{I}_i^{obj} \sum_{c \in classes} \left(p_i(c) - \hat{p}_i(c) \right)^2$$

Where

$\mathbb{I}_i^{obj}$ is 1 if an object is in cell i, or 0 otherwise.

$\hat{p}_i(c)$ denotes the probability of having class c in cell i.

Localization Loss

This loss measures the error of the predicted bounding boxes with respect to the expected ones.

$$\lambda_{coord} \sum_{i=0}^{S^2} \sum_{j=0}^{B} \mathbb{I}_i^{obj} \left[\left(x_i - \hat{x}_i \right)^2 + \left(y_i - \hat{y}_i \right)^2 \right] +$$

$$\lambda_{coord} \sum_{i=0}^{S^2} \sum_{j=0}^{B} \mathbb{I}_i^{obj} \left[\left(\sqrt{w_i} - \sqrt{\hat{w}_i} \right)^2 + \left(\sqrt{h_i} - \sqrt{\hat{h}_i} \right)^2 \right]$$

Confidence Loss

The confidence loss measures the error when deciding if an object is in the box or not.

$$\sum_{i=0}^{S^2} \sum_{j=0}^{B} \mathbb{I}_{ij}^{obj} \left(C_i - \hat{C}_i \right)^2$$

Where

$\hat{C}_i$ is the confidence of the box j in cell i.

$\mathbb{I}_{ij}^{obj}$ is 1 if the jth bounding box in cell i is responsible for detecting the object.

Since most cells does not contain an object, we must be careful. The network could learn that the background is important. We need to add a term to the cost function to remedy this. This is done with the additional term:

$$\lambda_{noobj} \sum_{i=0}^{S^2} \sum_{j=0}^{B} \mathbb{I}_{ij}^{noobj} \left(C_i - \hat{C}_i \right)^2$$

Where $\mathbb{I}_{ij}^{noobj}$ is the opposite of $\mathbb{I}_{ij}^{obj}$.

Total Loss Function

The total loss function is simply the sum of all the terms:

$$L = \sum_{i=0}^{S^2} \mathbb{I}_i^{obj} \sum_{c \in classes} \left(p_i(c) - \hat{p}_i(c) \right)^2 + \lambda_{coord} \sum_{i=0}^{S^2} \sum_{j=0}^{B} \mathbb{I}_i^{obj} \left[\left(x_i - \hat{x}_i \right)^2 + \left(y_i - \hat{y}_i \right)^2 \right] +$$

$$\lambda_{coord} \sum_{i=0}^{S^2} \sum_{j=0}^{B} \mathbb{I}_i^{obj} \left[\left(\sqrt{w_i} - \sqrt{\hat{w}_i} \right)^2 + \left(\sqrt{h_i} - \sqrt{\hat{h}_i} \right)^2 \right] +$$

$$\sum_{i=0}^{S^2} \sum_{j=0}^{B} \mathbb{I}_{ij}^{obj} \left(C_i - \hat{C}_i \right)^2 + \lambda_{noobj} \sum_{i=0}^{S^2} \sum_{j=0}^{B} \mathbb{I}_{ij}^{noobj} \left(C_i - \hat{C}_i \right)^2$$

As you can see, it's a complicated formula to implement. This is one of the reasons that the easiest way to do object detection is to download and use a pre-trained model. Starting from scratch will require some time and effort. Believe me.

In the next sections, we will look at how you can use YOLO algorithms (in particular, YOLOv3) in your own Python projects.

YOLO Implementation in Python and OpenCV

Darknet Implementation of YOLO

If you followed the previous sections, you understand that developing your own models for YOLO from scratch is not feasible for a beginner (and for almost all practitioners), so, as we have done in previous chapters, we need to use pre-trained models to use object detection in your projects. The web page where you can find all the pre-trained models you could ever want is `https://pjreddie.com`. This is the home page of Joseph C. Redmon, the maintainer of Darknet.

Note   Darknet is an open source neural network framework written in C and CUDA. It is fast, easy to install, and supports CPU and GPU computation.

On a subpage (`https://pjreddie.com/darknet/yolo/`), you will find all the information you need about the YOLO algorithm. You can download from this page the weights of several pre-trained models. For each model, you will always need two files:

- A `.cfg` file, which basically contains the structure of the network.

- A `.weights` file, which contains the weights obtained after training.

To give you an idea of the content of the files, the `.cfg` file contains, among other things, information on all the layers used. An example follows:

```
[convolutional]
batch_normalize=1
filters=64
size=3
```

```
stride=1
pad=1
activation=leaky
```

This tells you how that particular convolutional layer is structured. The most important information contained in the file is about:

- Network architecture

- Anchor boxes

- Number of classes

- Learning rate and other parameters used

- Batch size

The other file (`.weights`) contains the pre-trained weights that you need in order to perform inference. Note that they are not saved in a Keras compatible format (like the `.h5` files we have used so far), so they cannot be loaded in a Keras model unless you convert them first.

There is no standard tool or utility to convert those files, since the format is not constant (it has changed for example between YOLOv2 and YOLOv3). If you are interested in using YOLO up to v2, you can use the YAD2K library (Yet Another Darknet 2 Keras), which can be found at `https://github.com/allanzelener/YAD2K`.

Note that this does not work on YOLOv3 `.cfg` files. Believe me, I have tried. But if you are happy with YOLOv2, you can use the code in this repository to convert the `.weight` files into a more Keras-friendly format.

I also want to point out another GitHub repository that implemented a converter for YOLOv3 at `https://github.com/qqwweee/keras-yolo3`. It has some limitations (for example, you must use standard anchors), but it may be a good starting point to convert the files. However, there is an easier way to use the pre-trained models and that is using OpenCV, as we will see later in the chapter.

Testing Object Detection with Darknet

If you simply want to perform some classification on an image, the easiest way to do that is to follow the instructions on the darknet website. Let's look at how that works here. Note that the instructions work if you are on a Linux or MacOS X system. On Windows, you need to have make, gcc, and several other tools installed. As described on the website, the installation needs only a few lines:

```
git clone https://github.com/pjreddie/darknet
cd darknet
make
wget https://pjreddie.com/media/files/yolov3.weights
```

At this point, you can simply perform your object detection with this:[5]

```
./darknet detect cfg/yolov3.cfg yolov3.weights table.jpg
```

Note that the .weight file is very big (around 237MB). Keep that in mind when downloading it. On a CPU this is quite slow; it took a very modern MacBook Pro from 2018 18 seconds to download. You can see the result in Figure 7-2.

---

[5]You can find the image used for testing in the GitHub repository within Chapter 7.

Figure 7-2. *YOLOv3 used with darknet on a test image*

By default, a threshold of 0.25 is used. But you can specify a different one using the -thresh XYZ parameter. You must change XYZ to the threshold value you want to use.

This method is nice for playing with object detection, but it's difficult to use in your Python projects. To do that, you will need to be able to use the pre-trained models in your code. There are several ways to do that, but the easiest way is to use the opencv library. If you are working with images, chances are that you are already working with this library. If you have never heard of it, I strongly suggest you check it out, since it's a great library for working with images. You can find the official web page at https:// opencv.org.

You can, as usual, find the entire code in the GitHub repository, within the Chapter 7 folder of this book. We will discuss only the most important parts for brevity.

You will need to have the newest opencv library installed. The code we discuss here has been developed with version 4.1.0. To determine which version you have, use this:

```
import cv2
print (cv2.__version__)
```

To try the code we discuss here, you need three files from the https:// pjreddie.com website:

- coco.names

- yolov3.cfg

- yolov3.weights

coco.names contains the labels of the classes that the pre-trained model can classify. The yolov3.cfg and yolov3.weights files contain the model configuration parameters (as we have discussed) and the weights we need to use. For your convenience, since the yolov3.weights is about 240MB and cannot be uploaded to GitHub, you can download a ZIP file of all three at http://toe.lt/r. In the code, we need to specify where the files are. For example, you can use the following code:

```
weightsPath = "yolo-coco/yolov3.weights"
configPath = "yolo-coco/yolov3.cfg"
```

You need to change the location to where you saved the files on your system. OpenCV provides a function to load the weights without the need to convert them:

```
net = cv2.dnn.readNetFromDarknet(configPath, weightsPath)
```

This is quite confortable, since you don't need to analyze or write your own loading function. It returns a model object that we will use later for inference. If you remember from the discussion about the method at the beginning of the chapter, we need to get the output layers, in order to get all the information we need, like bounding boxes or predicted classes. We can do that easily with the following code:

```
ln = net.getLayerNames()
ln = [ln[i[0] - 1] for i in net.getUnconnectedOutLayers()]
```

The getUnconnectedOutLayers() function returns indexes of layers with unconnected outputs, which is exactly what we are looking for. The ln variable will contain the following layers:

```
['yolo_82', 'yolo_94', 'yolo_106']
```

Then we need to resize the image in a square 416x416 image and normalize it by dividing the pixel values by 255.0:

```
blob = cv2.dnn.blobFromImage(image, 1 / 255.0, (416, 416),
swapRB=True, crop=False)
```

Then we need to use it as input to our model saved in the net model:

```
net.setInput(blob)
```

And then we can use the forward() call to do a forward pass-through of the pre-trained model:

```
layerOutputs = net.forward(ln)
```

We are not yet done, so don't relax. We need to extract the bounding boxes, which we will save in the boxes list, then the confidences, saved in the confidences list, and then the predicted classes, saved in the classIDs list.

We first initialize the lists as follows:

```
boxes = []
confidences = []
classIDs = []
```

Then we loop over the layers and extract the information we need. We can perform the loops as follows:

```
for output in layerOutputs:
    for detection in output:
```

Now the scores are saved in the elements starting from the fifth in the detection variable, and we can extract the predicted class with np.argmax(scores):

```
scores = detection[5:]
classID = np.argmax(scores)
```

The confidence is of course the score of the predicted class:

```
confidence = scores[classID]
```

We want to keep predictions with a confidence bigger than zero. In the code used here, we chose a limit of 0.15. The predicted bounding box is contained in the first four values of the detection variable:

```
box = detection[0:4] * np.array([W, H, W, H])
(centerX, centerY, width, height) = box.astype("int")
```

And if you remember, YOLO predicts the center of the bounding box, so we need to extract the upper-left corner position:

```
x = int(centerX - (width / 2))
y = int(centerY - (height / 2))
```

And then we can simply append the found values to the lists:

```
boxes.append([x, y, int(width), int(height)])
confidences.append(float(confidence))
classIDs.append(classID)
```

Then we need to use non-maxima suppression (as discussed in the previous sections). OpenCV provides also a function[6] for it:

```
idxs = cv2.dnn.NMSBoxes(boxes, confidences, 0.6,0.2)
```

The function needs the following parameters:

- A set of bounding boxes (saved in the boxes variable)

- A set of confidences (saved in the confidences variable)

- A threshold used to filter boxes by score (0.6 in the previous code)

- The threshold used in non-maximum suppression (the 0.2 in the previous code)

Then we can obtain the right coordinates with this simple code:

```
for i in idxs.flatten():
        # extract the bounding box coordinates
        (x, y) = (boxes[i][0], boxes[i][1])
        (w, h) = (boxes[i][2], boxes[i][3])
```

You can see in Figure 7-3 the results of this code.

---

[6]You can find the official documentation at http://toe.lt/t.

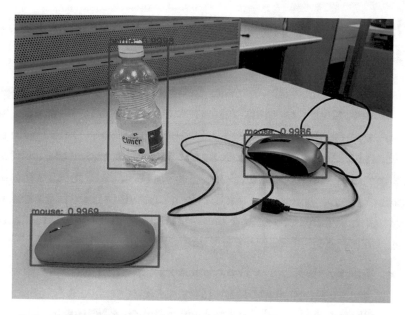

Figure 7-3. *YOLOv3 results obtained with OpenCV*

That is exactly as it should be—the same results as in Figure 7-2. In addition, we have the probability of the prediction on the box. You can see how easy this is. You simply add those few lines of code to your project.

Keep in mind that the model we built using the pre-trained weights will only detect the objects that are contained in the image dataset that the pre-trained model has been trained with. If you need to use the model on different objects, you need to fine-tune the models, or train it from scratch for your objects. Describing how to train the model completely from scratch is beyond the scope of the book, but in the next section, I provide some pointers in case you need to do it.

Training a Model for YOLO for Your Specific Images

I will not describe the different procedures you need to train your own YOLO models, since that would take a few chapters on its own, but I hope I can point you in the right direction. Let's suppose you want to train a model specifically for your images. As a first step, you need the training data. Supposing you have enough images, you first need to label them. Remember that you need to mark the right bounding boxes for each image. Doing that manually is an almost impossible task, so I suggest two projects that will help you label your training data.

- *BBox-Label-Tool by Darkflow Annotations*: This tool can be found at `https://github.com/enriqueav/BBox-Label-Tool`. The tool saves the annotations in the right format as expected by Darkflow (a Python wrapper that can use darknet weight files, `https://github.com/thtrieu/darkflow`).

- *labelImg*: This tool can be found at `https://github.com/tzutalin/labelImg`. This tool can be used with several Python installations (including Anaconda, for example) and on several operating systems (including Windows).

Check them out in case you want to try to train your YOLO model on your data. Since describing the entire procedure would go well beyond the scope of the book, I suggest you read the following medium post, which does quite a good job at describing how to do that: `http://toe.lt/v`. Remember that you need to modify a `cfg` file so that you can specify the right number of classes that you are trying to identify. For example, in the `yolov3.cfg` file, you will find this line (at line 610):

```
classes=80
```

It tells you how many classes you can identify with the models. You will need to modify this line to reflect the number of classes you have in your problem.

On the official YOLO website, there is a detailed description of how to do that: `https://pjreddie.com/darknet/yolo/`. Scroll down until you find the sections on training the models with your own datasets. Do not underestimate the complexity of this task. Lots of reading and testing will be required.

Concluding Remarks

As you might have noticed, using these advanced techniques is quite complicated and not simply a matter of copying a few lines of code. You need to make sure you understand how the algorithms work to be able to use them in your own projects. Depending on the object you need to detect, you may need to spend quite some time building a custom model suited for your problem. That will require lots of testing and coding. It will not be easy. My goal with this chapter was to give you enough tools to help you and point you in the right direction.

After the previous chapters, you have now enough understanding of advanced techniques to be able to re-implement even complicated algorithms as YOLO on your own, although this will require time and effort. You will suffer a lot, but if you don't give up, you will be rewarded with success. I am sure of it.

In the next chapter, we look at a complete example that uses CNNs on real data, where we use all the techniques that we have learned so far. Consider Chapter 8 as an exercise. Try to play with the data and reproduce the results described there. I hope you have fun!

CHAPTER 8

Histology Tissue Classification

Now it's time to put all we have learned together and see how the techniques we have learned so far can be used on a real dataset. We will use a dataset that I have used successfully as my end project in my university course on deep learning: the "collection of textures in colorectal cancer histology".[1] This dataset can be found on several websites:

- `http://toe.lt/f`: On `zenodo.org`

- `http://toe.lt/g`: On Kaggle (this dataset was prepared originally by Kevin Mäder[2] and me for the purpose of the university course we held during the Autumn semester of 2018 at the Zürich University of Applied Science)

- `http://toe.lt/h`: Since TensorFlow 2.0, this is also available as a pre-read dataset (the link points to the TensorFlow GitHub repository for the dataset's API)

---

[1]Kather JN, Weis CA, Bianconi F, Melchers SM, Schad LR, Gaiser T, Marx A, Zollner *F: Multi-class texture analysis in colorectal cancer histology* (2016), *Scientific Reports* (in press)

[2]`https://www.linkedin.com/in/kevinmader/`

Don't download the data yet. I prepared a *pickle* (more on that later) file for you with all the data ready to be used. You will find all the information in the next section.

The thing we will use in this chapter is the `Kather_texture_2016_image_tiles_5000` folder and it contains 5000 histological images of 150x150px each (74x74µm). Each image belongs to exactly one of eight tissue categories (specified by the folder name from the Zenodo website). In the code, I assume that, within the folder where you have your Jupyter Notebooks, you have a `data` folder and under that `data` folder, you have the `Kather_texture_2016_image_tiles_5000` folder.

In the GitHub repository for this book, the folder for Chapter 8 contains the complete code that you can use. In this chapter, we will look only at the parts that are relevant to our discussions. If you want to try this, please use the GitHub repository. The code is complete and directly usable. The goal of this project is to build a classifier that can classify the different images into one of eight classes. We will look at them in the next sections and see where the difficulties are. Let's start, as usual, with the data.

Most of the code was developed by Fabien Tarrade (`https://www.linkedin.com/in/fabientarrade/`) for my university course, and he was nice enough to give me permission to use it. I have updated it quite a bit to make it usable in this example. Note that everything that works is thanks to Fabien, and all the bugs are my fault.

Data Analysis and Preparation

The code for this section is contained in the notebook called `01- Data exploration and preparation.ipynb`, which is in the book's GitHub repository in the Chapter 8 folder. Feel free to follow this discussion with a window open on your computer to try the code. Since we have the images in different folders, we need to load them in a pandas dataframe and automatically generate a label from the folder name. For example, the image

1A11_CRC-Prim-HE-07_022.tif_Row_601_Col_151.tif is contained in the folder 01_TUMOR and therefore must have "TUMOR" as its label.

We can automate that process in a very simple way. We start with this code (for all the imports, please check the code in GitHub):

```
df = pd.DataFrame({'path': glob(os.path.join(base_dir, '*',
'*.tif'))})
```

This generates a dataframe with just one column, 'path'. This column contains the path to each image we want to load. The base_dir variable contains the path to the Kather_texture_2016_image_tiles_5000 folder. For example, I am running the code in Google Colab and my base_dir looks like this:

```
base_dir = '/content/drive/My Drive/Book2-ch8/data/Kather_
texture_2016_image_tiles_5000'
```

The first five records of my dataframe look like this:

```
/content/drive/My Drive/Book2-ch8/data/Kather_texture_2016_
image_tiles_5000/05_DEBRIS/5434_CRC-Prim-HE-04_002.tif_Row_451_
Col_1351.tif
/content/drive/My Drive/Book2-ch8/data/Kather_texture_2016_
image_tiles_5000/05_DEBRIS/626A_CRC-Prim-HE-08_024.tif_Row_451_
Col_1.tif
/content/drive/My Drive/Book2-ch8/data/Kather_texture_2016_
image_tiles_5000/05_DEBRIS/148A7_CRC-Prim-HE-04_004.tif_
Row_151_Col_901.tif
/content/drive/My Drive/Book2-ch8/data/Kather_texture_2016_
image_tiles_5000/05_DEBRIS/6B37_CRC-Prim-HE-08_024.tif_
Row_1501_Col_301.tif
/content/drive/My Drive/Book2-ch8/data/Kather_texture_2016_
image_tiles_5000/05_DEBRIS/6B44_CRC-Prim-HE-03_010.tif_Row_301_
Col_451.tif
```

Now we can use the `.map()` function to extract all the information we need and create new columns.

```
df['file_id'] = df['path'].map(lambda x: os.path.splitext(os.
path.basename(x))[0])
df['cell_type'] = df['path'].map(lambda x: os.path.basename(os.
path.dirname(x)))
df['cell_type_idx'] = df['cell_type'].map(lambda x: int(x.
split('_')[0]))
df['cell_type'] = df['cell_type'].map(lambda x: x.split('_')[1])
df['full_image_name'] = df['file_id'].map(lambda x: x.split('_
Row')[0])
df['full_image_row'] = df['file_id'].map(lambda x: int(x.
split('_')[-3]))
df['full_image_col'] = df['file_id'].map(lambda x: int(x.
split('_')[-1]))
```

You can easily check what each call is doing. The column name should tell you what you will have in each column. In Figure 8-1, you can see the first two records of the dataframe so far.

	path	file_id	cell_type	cell_type_idx	full_image_name	full_image_row	full_image_col
0	ch8/data/Kather_texture_2016_image_tiles_5000/05_DEBRIS/5434_CRC-Prim-HE-04_002.tif_Row_451_Col_1351.tif	/content/drive/My Drive/Book2-5434_CRC-Prim-HE-04_002.tif_Row_451_Col_1351	DEBRIS	5	5434_CRC-Prim-HE-04_002.tif	451	1351
1	ch8/data/Kather_texture_2016_image_tiles_5000/05_DEBRIS/626A_CRC-Prim-HE-08_024.tif_Row_451_Col_1.tif	/content/drive/My Drive/Book2-626A_CRC-Prim-HE-08_024.tif_Row_451_Col_1	DEBRIS	5	626A_CRC-Prim-HE-08_024.tif	451	1

Figure 8-1. *The first two records of the dataframe df before loading the images*

At this point, we must read the images with `imread()`. To do this, we can simply use

```
df['image'] = df['path'].map(imread)
```

Keep in mind that this can take some time (depending on where you are running it). This will create a new column called `image` that will contain the images. For your convenience, I used the `to_pickle()` pandas call to save the dataframe to disk. *Pickling* is the process whereby a Python object hierarchy is converted into a byte stream[3] and then can be saved on-disk. The file is called `dataframe_Kather_texture_2016_image_tiles_5000.pkl`. You can load it with:

```
df=pd.read_pickle('/content/drive/My Drive/Book2-ch8/data/
dataframe_Kather_texture_2016_image_tiles_5000.pkl')
```

This way, you can save yourself lots of time. You don't even need to download the data since you can simply use the pickle I prepared for you. Note that the pickles are too big for GitHub, so I saved them on a server where you can download them. You will find the links in GitHub and at the end of this section. First things first: what classes do we have in this dataset? We can check the labels we have with this code:

```
df['cell_type'].unique()
```

This will give us the following:

```
array(['DEBRIS', 'ADIPOSE', 'LYMPHO', 'EMPTY', 'STROMA', 'TUMOR',
       'MUCOSA', 'COMPLEX'], dtype=object)
```

So here are our eight classes. We have 5000 images, which we can check using this:

```
df.shape
```

It gives us this:

```
(5000, 8)
```

---

[3]From the official Python documentation: `https://docs.python.org/2/library/pickle.html`

The next step is to check if we have a balanced class distribution. We can count how many images we have for each class:

```
df['cell_type'].value_counts()
```

Luckily, we have exactly 625 images for each class.

```
EMPTY        625
ADIPOSE      625
STROMA       625
COMPLEX      625
LYMPHO       625
DEBRIS       625
TUMOR        625
MUCOSA       625
Name: cell_type, dtype: int64
```

Strangely enough, there are five duplicate images. You can check that with this code:

```
df['full_image_name'][df.duplicated('full_image_name')]
```

This will report the names of the images that appear twice. You can see them in Figure 8-2. Since there are only five, we will simply ignore this problem.

Figure 8-2. *Five images appear twice in the dataset*

In Figure 8-3, you can see a few examples of each class.

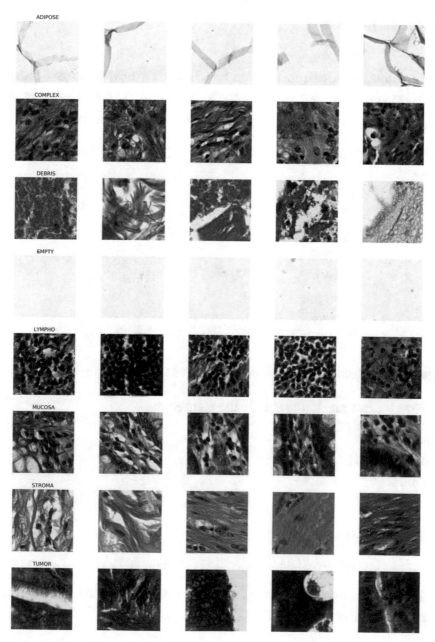

Figure 8-3. *Examples of the images in each class*

As expected, each image has a size of $(150, 150, 3)$:

```
df['image'][0].shape
(150, 150, 3)
```

Note how the classes are ordered, which is due to how we loaded the data. The DEBRIS class comes first, then ADIPOSE, and so on. This can be checked using a plot of the class label versus the index, as you can see in Figure 8-4.

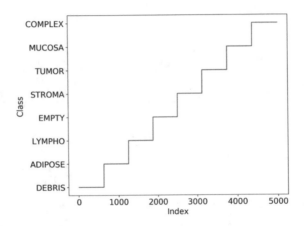

Figure 8-4. *A plot showing how the images in the dataframe are ordered*

Now we can randomly shuffle the elements:

```
import random
rows = df.index.values
random.shuffle(rows)
print(rows)
```

That will give you

```
array([1115, 4839, 3684, ...,  187, 1497, 2375])
```

You can see that the indexes are now randomly shuffled. The last step we need to take is to modify the actual dataframe:

```
df=df.reindex(rows)
df.sort_index(inplace=True)
```

At this point, the elements are shuffled. Now we need to one-hot-encode the labels. Pandas provide a very useful and easy-to-use method for this process:

```
df_label = pd.get_dummies(df['cell_type'])
```

It will give you one-hot-encoded labels, as you can see from Figure 8-5.

	ADIPOSE	COMPLEX	DEBRIS	EMPTY	LYMPHO	MUCOSA	STROMA	TUMOR
0	0	1	0	0	0	0	0	0
1	0	0	0	0	1	0	0	0
2	0	0	0	0	0	1	0	0
3	0	0	0	0	0	0	1	0
4	0	0	0	1	0	0	0	0

Figure 8-5. *The result of using the get_dummies() pandas function to one-hot-encode labels*

There are a few steps that we need to use the data with Keras. One is that we need to transform the dataframe to a numpy array:

```
data=np.array(df['image'].tolist())
```

Then, as usual, we need to create a training, test, and development dataset to make all the usual checks:

```
x, x_test, y, y_test = train_test_split(data, label, test_
size=0.2,train_size=0.8)
x_train, x_val, y_train, y_val = train_test_split(x, y, test_
size = 0.25,train_size =0.75)
```

You can check the dimensions of the three datasets easily with this code:

```
print('1- Training set:', x_train.shape, y_train.shape)
print('2- Validation set:', x_val.shape, y_val.shape)
print('3- Testing set:', x_test.shape, y_test.shape)
```

That should give you the following:

```
1- Training set: (3000, 150, 150, 3) (3000, 8)
2- Validation set: (1000, 150, 150, 3) (1000, 8)
3- Testing set: (1000, 150, 150, 3) (1000, 8)
```

Now you will see that the data is of type integer. We need to cast them to floating point numbers since we want to normalize them later. To do that, we use this code:

```
x_train = np.array(x_train, dtype=np.float32)
x_test = np.array(x_test, dtype=np.float32)
x_val = np.array( x_val, dtype=np.float32)
```

Then we can normalize the datasets (remember that each pixel will have a maximum value of 255):

```
x_train /= 255.0
x_test /= 255.0
x_val /= 255.0
```

For your convenience, I saved all the prepared datasets as pickles. If you want to follow from here and play with the data, you need to load the pickles using the following commands (you will need to change the folder name where the files are saved):

```
x_train=pickle.load(open('/content/drive/My Drive/Book2-ch8/
data/x_train.pkl', 'rb'))
x_test=pickle.load(open('/content/drive/My Drive/Book2-ch8/
data/x_test.pkl', 'rb'))
x_val=pickle.load(open('/content/drive/My Drive/Book2-ch8/
data/x_val.pkl', 'rb'))
y_train=pickle.load(open('/content/drive/My Drive/Book2-ch8/
data/y_train.pkl', 'rb'))
y_test=pickle.load(open('/content/drive/My Drive/Book2-ch8/
data/y_test.pkl', 'rb'))
y_val=pickle.load(open('/content/drive/My Drive/Book2-ch8/
data/y_val.pkl', 'rb'))
```

You will then have everything ready. Keep in mind that the files containing the data (x_train, x_test, and x_val) are big files, with x_train being 800MB unzipped. Keep that in mind if you plan to download the files or upload them on your Google drive. Of course, you will need to change the folder to where your data is saved. This will save you time. Pickles are usually saved, since you don't want to rerun the entire data preparation each time you experiment with the data. In the 01- Data exploration and preparation. ipynb files, you will also find some histogram analysis and data augmentation examples. For space reasons and to keep this chapter compact, we will not look at histogram analysis, but we will talk about data augmentation later in the chapter, as it's a very effective way of fighting overfitting.

The files were too big for GitHub, so I put them on a server where you can download them. In the GitHub repository (the Chapter 8 folder), you will find all the information. If you don't have access to GitHub and you still want to download the files, here are the links:

- dataframe_Kather_texture_201_image_tiles_5000. pkl (340MB unzipped): http://toe.lt/j

- x_test.pkl (270MB unzipped): http://toe.lt/k

- x_train.pkl (810MB unzipped): http://toe.lt/m

- x_val.pkl (270MB unzipped): http://toe.lt/n

- y_train, y_test, and y_val (all zipped together) (about 50KB unzipped): http://toe.lt/p

Model Building

It is time to build some models. You will find all the code in the book's GitHub repository (Chapter 8 folder, in the 02_Model_building.ipynb notebook), so we will not look at all the details here. The best way to follow along is to keep the notebook open and try the code while you are reading this. As mentioned, we first need to load the pickle files. We can do that with the following code:

```
x_train=pickle.load(open(base_dir+'x_train.pkl', 'rb'))
x_test=pickle.load(open(base_dir+'x_test.pkl', 'rb'))
x_val=pickle.load(open(base_dir+'x_val.pkl', 'rb'))
y_train=pickle.load(open(base_dir+'y_train.pkl', 'rb'))
y_test=pickle.load(open(base_dir+'y_test.pkl', 'rb'))
y_val=pickle.load(open(base_dir+'y_val.pkl', 'rb'))
```

Then we need to define the input_shape variable that we will need for our CNNs. In the code we always define functions that return the Keras models. For example, our first try looks like this:

```
def model_cnn_v1():

    # must define the input shape in the first layer of the
    neural network
    model = tf.keras.models.Sequential()
    model.add(tf.keras.layers.Conv2D(32, 3, 3, input_
    shape=input_shape))
    model.add(tf.keras.layers.Activation('relu'))
    model.add(tf.keras.layers.MaxPooling2D(pool_size=(2, 2)))

    model.add(tf.keras.layers.Conv2D(64, 3, 3))
    model.add(tf.keras.layers.Activation('relu'))
    model.add(tf.keras.layers.MaxPooling2D(pool_size=(2, 2)))

    model.add(tf.keras.layers.Flatten())
    model.add(tf.keras.layers.Dense(64))
    model.add(tf.keras.layers.Activation('relu'))
    model.add(tf.keras.layers.Dropout(0.5))
    model.add(tf.keras.layers.Dense(8))
    model.add(tf.keras.layers.Activation('sigmoid'))

    model.compile(loss='categorical_crossentropy',
                  optimizer='adam',
                  metrics=['accuracy'])
    return model
```

This is a simple network, as you can check with the summary() function:

Layer (type)	Output Shape	Param #
conv2d (Conv2D)	(None, 50, 50, 32)	896
activation (Activation)	(None, 50, 50, 32)	0
max_pooling2d (MaxPooling2D)	(None, 25, 25, 32)	0
conv2d_1 (Conv2D)	(None, 8, 8, 64)	18496
activation_1 (Activation)	(None, 8, 8, 64)	0
max_pooling2d_1 (MaxPooling2	(None, 4, 4, 64)	0
flatten (Flatten)	(None, 1024)	0
dense (Dense)	(None, 64)	65600
activation_2 (Activation)	(None, 64)	0
dropout (Dropout)	(None, 64)	0
dense_1 (Dense)	(None, 8)	520
activation_3 (Activation)	(None, 8)	0

Total params: 85,512
Trainable params: 85,512
Non-trainable params: 0

To make sure that the session is reset, we always use:

```
tf.keras.backend.clear_session()
```

Then we create an instance of the model, as follows:

```
model_cnn_v1=model_cnn_v1()
```

Then we also save the initial weights to make sure, if we do runs later, that we start from these same weights:

```
initial_weights = model_cnn_v1.get_weights()
```

Then we train the model with this:

```
model_cnn_v1.set_weights(initial_weights)
# define path to save the mnodel
path_model=base_dir+'model_cnn_v1.weights.best.hdf5'
shutil.rmtree(path_model, ignore_errors=True)

checkpointer = ModelCheckpoint(filepath=path_model,
                               verbose = 1,
                               save_best_only=True)
EPOCHS=200
BATCH_SIZE=256

history=model_cnn_v1.fit(x_train,
                         y_train,
                         batch_size=BATCH_SIZE,
                         epochs=EPOCHS,
                         validation_data=(x_test, y_test),
                         callbacks=[checkpointer])
```

Note a few points:

- We create a custom CallBack class `ModelCheckpoint`, which will save the weights of the network during training every time the loss functions diminishes.

- We train the network with the `fit()` call and save its output in a `history` variable, to be able to plot loss and metrics later.

Note   Training such networks may be very slow if you do it on your laptop or desktop, depending on the hardware you have. I strongly suggest you do that on Google Colab, since this will speed up your testing. All the notebooks in the book's GitHub repository have been tested on Google Colab and can be opened in Google Colab directly from GitHub.

On Google Colab, training the previous network will take roughly three minutes. It will reach the following accuracies:

- Accuracy on the training dataset: 85%

- Accuracy on the validation dataset: 82.7%

These results are not bad, and we don't have much overfitting (you can see in Figure 8-6 how accuracy and loss change with the epochs).

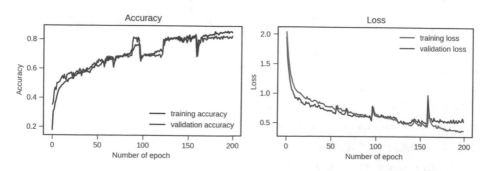

Figure 8-6. *Accuracy and loss function for the first network described in the text*

257

Let's move to a different model, which we will call v2. This one has a lot more parameters than the previous one:

Layer (type)	Output Shape	Param #
conv2d (Conv2D)	(None, 150, 150, 128)	9728
max_pooling2d (MaxPooling2D)	(None, 75, 75, 128)	0
dropout (Dropout)	(None, 75, 75, 128)	0
conv2d_1 (Conv2D)	(None, 75, 75, 64)	73792
max_pooling2d_1 (MaxPooling2	(None, 37, 37, 64)	0
dropout_1 (Dropout)	(None, 37, 37, 64)	0
conv2d_2 (Conv2D)	(None, 37, 37, 64)	36928
max_pooling2d_2 (MaxPooling2	(None, 18, 18, 64)	0
dropout_2 (Dropout)	(None, 18, 18, 64)	0
flatten (Flatten)	(None, 20736)	0
dense (Dense)	(None, 256)	5308672
dense_1 (Dense)	(None, 64)	16448
dense_2 (Dense)	(None, 32)	2080
dense_3 (Dense)	(None, 8)	264

Total params: 5,447,912
Trainable params: 5,447,912
Non-trainable params: 0

Again, you can find all the code in the GitHub repository. We will train it again, but this time, for time reasons, for 50 epochs and with a slightly smaller batch size of 64.

```
EPOCHS=50
BATCH_SIZE=64

history=model_cnn_v2.fit(x_train,
                         y_train,
                         batch_size=BATCH_SIZE,
                         epochs=EPOCHS,
                         validation_data=(x_test, y_test),
                         callbacks=[checkpointer])
```

Otherwise, everything remains the same. This time, due to the sheer number of parameters, you will notice that we get an evident overfitting. In fact, we get the following accuracies:

- Accuracy on the training dataset: 99.5%

- Accuracy on the validation dataset: 74%

You can clearly see the overfitting in Figure 8-7, looking at the plot of the accuracies versus the number of epochs.

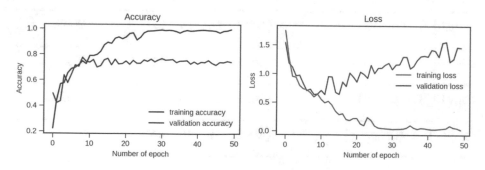

Figure 8-7. *Accuracies and loss functions versus the number of epochs for the v2 network*

We need to work a bit more to get some more reasonable results. Now let's use a network with fewer parameters (in particular, with fewer kernels):

Layer (type)	Output Shape	Param #
conv2d (Conv2D)	(None, 150, 150, 16)	448
conv2d_1 (Conv2D)	(None, 150, 150, 16)	2320
conv2d_2 (Conv2D)	(None, 150, 150, 16)	2320
dropout (Dropout)	(None, 150, 150, 16)	0
max_pooling2d (MaxPooling2D)	(None, 50, 50, 16)	0
conv2d_3 (Conv2D)	(None, 50, 50, 32)	4640
conv2d_4 (Conv2D)	(None, 50, 50, 32)	9248
conv2d_5 (Conv2D)	(None, 50, 50, 32)	9248
dropout_1 (Dropout)	(None, 50, 50, 32)	0
max_pooling2d_1 (MaxPooling2	(None, 16, 16, 32)	0
conv2d_6 (Conv2D)	(None, 16, 16, 64)	18496
conv2d_7 (Conv2D)	(None, 16, 16, 64)	36928
conv2d_8 (Conv2D)	(None, 16, 16, 64)	36928
dropout_2 (Dropout)	(None, 16, 16, 64)	0

max_pooling2d_2 (MaxPooling2	(None, 5, 5, 64)	0
conv2d_9 (Conv2D)	(None, 5, 5, 128)	73856
conv2d_10 (Conv2D)	(None, 5, 5, 128)	147584
conv2d_11 (Conv2D)	(None, 5, 5, 256)	295168
dropout_3 (Dropout)	(None, 5, 5, 256)	0
max_pooling2d_3 (MaxPooling2	(None, 1, 1, 256)	0
global_max_pooling2d (Global	(None, 256)	0
dense (Dense)	(None, 8)	2056

```
=================================================================
Total params: 639,240
Trainable params: 639,240
Non-trainable params: 0
```

We will call this network v3. This time, the situation is not much better, as you can see in Figure 8-8.

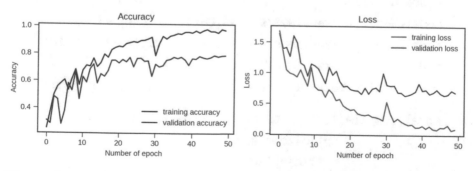

Figure 8-8. *Accuracies and loss functions versus. the number of epochs for the v3 network.*

Why don't we use what we have learned so far? Let's use transfer learning and see if we can use a pre-trained network. Let's download the VGG16 network and retrain the last layers with our data. To do that, we need to use the following code (we will call this network vgg-v4):

```python
def model_vgg16_v4():

    # load the VGG model
    vgg_conv = tf.keras.applications.VGG16(weights='imagenet',
include_top=False, input_shape = input_shape)

    # freeze the layers except the last 4 layers
    for layer in vgg_conv.layers[:-4]:
            layer.trainable = False

    # Check the trainable status of the individual layers
    for layer in vgg_conv.layers:
        print(layer, layer.trainable)

    # create the model
    model = tf.keras.models.Sequential()

    # add the vgg convolutional base model
    model.add(vgg_conv)

    # add new layers
    model.add(tf.keras.layers.Flatten())
    model.add(tf.keras.layers.Dense(1024, activation='relu'))
    model.add(tf.keras.layers.Dropout(0.5))
    model.add(tf.keras.layers.Dense(8, activation='softmax'))

    model.compile(loss='categorical_crossentropy',
                  optimizer='adam',
                  metrics=['accuracy'])

    return model
```

Note how we downloaded the pre-trained network (as we have seen in previous chapters) with this code:

```
vgg_conv = tf.keras.applications.VGG16(weights='imagenet',
include_top=False, input_shape = input_shape)
```

We used the include_top=False parameter, since we want to remove the final dense layers and put our own in their place. We add a layer with 1024 neurons at the end:

```
model.add(tf.keras.layers.Dense(1024, activation='relu'))
```

Then we add an output layer with 8 as the softmax activation function for classification:

```
model.add(tf.keras.layers.Dense(8, activation='softmax'))
```

The summary() call will give you this overview:

Layer (type)	Output Shape	Param #
vgg16 (Model)	(None, 4, 4, 512)	14714688
flatten (Flatten)	(None, 8192)	0
dense (Dense)	(None, 1024)	8389632
dropout (Dropout)	(None, 1024)	0
dense_1 (Dense)	(None, 8)	8200

```
Total params: 23,112,520
Trainable params: 15,477,256
Non-trainable params: 7,635,264
```

The entire vgg16 network is condensed into one line (vgg16 (Model)). In this network, we have 15'477'256 trainable parameters. Quite a few. In fact, training this network for 30 epochs will require around 11 minutes on Google Colab. You can see in Figure 8-9 how accuracy and loss change with the number of epochs.

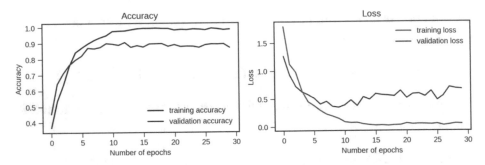

Figure 8-9. *Accuracies and loss functions versus the number of epochs for the vgg-v4 network*

As you can see, the situation is better, but we still get overfitting. It's not as dramatic as before, but still quite noticeable. The only strategy we have to fight this is data augmentation. In the next sections, we'll see how easy it is to do data augmentation in Keras and the effects it has.

Data Augmentation

One obvious strategy to fight overfitting (although one that is rarely doable in real life) is to get more training data. In our case here, this is not possible. The images given are the only ones available. But we can still do something in this case: *data augmentation*. What do we mean by that exactly? Typically, data augmentation consists of generating new images from existing ones by applying some kind of transformation to them and using them as additional training data.

Note   Data augmentation consists of generating new images from existing ones by applying some kind of transformation to them and using them as additional training data.

The most common transformations are as follows:

- Shifting the image by a certain number of pixels horizontally or vertically

- Rotating the image

- Changing its brightness

- Changing the zoom

- Changing the contrast

- Shearing the image[4]

Let's see how to do data augmentation in Keras, and let's look at a few examples in our dataset. The function we need to use is `ImageDataGenerator`. To start, you need to import it from `keras_preprocessing.image`:

```
from keras_preprocessing.image import ImageDataGenerator
```

Note that this function will not generate new images and save them to disk, but will create augmented image data for you just-in-time during the training in random fashion (later it will become clear how to use it). This will not require much additional memory, but will add

---

[4]In plane geometry, a *shear mapping* is a linear map that displaces each point in a fixed direction, by an amount proportional to its signed distance from the line that is parallel to that direction and goes through the origin. See `https://en.wikipedia.org/wiki/Shear_mapping`.

some additional time during model training. The function can do lots of transformations and the best way to discover them all is to look at the official documentation at `https://keras.io/preprocessing/image/`. We will look at the most important ones with examples.

Horizontal and Vertical Shifts

To shift images horizontally and vertically, you use the following code:

```
datagen = ImageDataGenerator(width_shift_range=.2,
                             height_shift_range=.2,
                             fill_mode='nearest')

# fit parameters from data
datagen.fit(x_train)
```

The result is shown in a few random images in Figure 8-10.

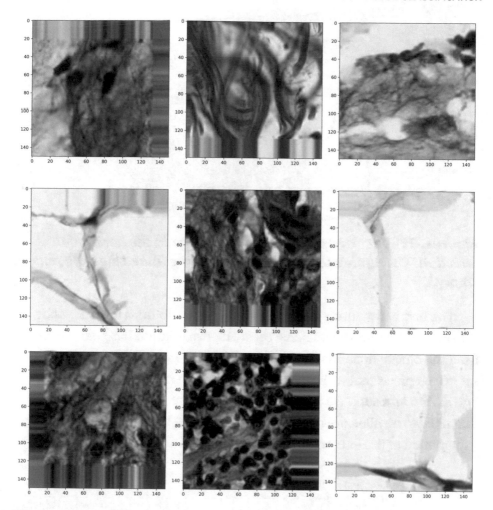

Figure 8-10. *The result of shifting images horizontally and vertically*

If you check the images, you will notice how strange features appear at the borders. Since we are shifting the image, we need to tell Keras how to fill the part of the image that remains empty. Consider Figure 8-11, where we shift an image horizontally. As you may notice, the part marked in the image with the A remains empty, and we can tell Keras how to fill that part using the fill_mode parameter.

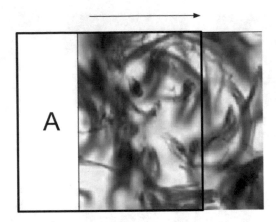

Figure 8-11. *An example of shifting an image in the horizontal direction. The A marks the part of the resulting image that will remain empty.*

The best way to understand the different possibilities for fill_mode is to consider a one-dimensional case. The explanation has been taken from the official documentation of the function. Let's suppose we have a set of four pixels that will have some values that we indicate with a, b, c, and d. And let's suppose we have boundaries that we need to fill. The parts that need to be filled are marked with o. Figure 8-12 shows a graphical explanation of the four possibilities: constant, nearest, reflect, and wrap.

	← BOUNDARY TO FILL →												← BOUNDARY TO FILL →							
	O	O	O	O	O	O	O	O	A	B	C	D	O	O	O	O	O	O	O	O
CONSTANT	K	K	K	K	K	K	K	K	A	B	C	D	K	K	K	K	K	K	K	K
NEAREST	A	A	A	A	A	A	A	A	A	B	C	D	D	D	D	D	D	D	D	D
REFLECT	A	B	C	D	D	C	B	A	A	B	C	D	D	C	B	A	A	B	C	D
WRAP	A	B	C	D	A	B	C	D	A	B	C	D	A	B	C	D	A	B	C	D

Figure 8-12. *Possible values for the fill_mode parameter and a graphical explanation of the possibilities*

The images in Figure 8-11 have been generated using the nearest fill mode. Although this transformation introduces artificial features, using those additional images for training increases the accuracy of the model and fights overfitting extremely effectively, as we will see later in the chapter. The most common method to fill the empty parts is nearest.

Flipping Images Vertically

To flip images vertically, the following code can be used:

```
datagen = ImageDataGenerator(vertical_flip=True)

# fit parameters from data
datagen.fit(x_train)
```

Randomly Rotating Images

You can randomly rotate images with this code:

```
datagen = ImageDataGenerator(rotation_range=40, fill_mode =
'constant')

# fit parameters from data
datagen.fit(x_train)
```

And, as with the shifting transformation, you can choose different ways of filling the empty areas. You can see the effect of this code in Figure 8-13.

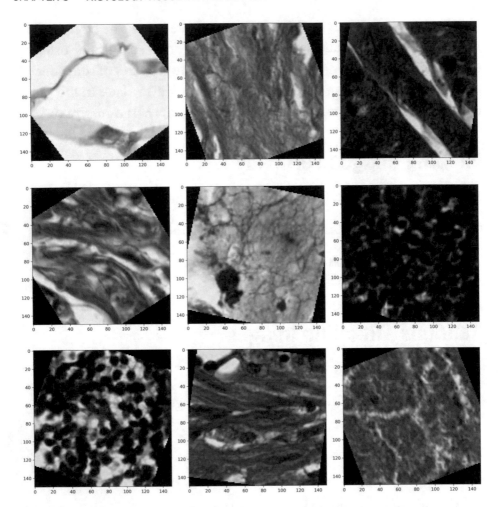

Figure 8-13. *The effect of rotating images in a random direction up to 40 degrees (the amount of rotation is chosen randomly up to 40 degrees). The parts of the images left empty by the rotation have been filled with a constant value.*

In Figure 8-14, you can see the effect of the rotation when it's filled with `fill_mode = 'nearest'`. Typically, this is the preferred way to fill the images to avoid giving black (or solid color) parts of images to the network.

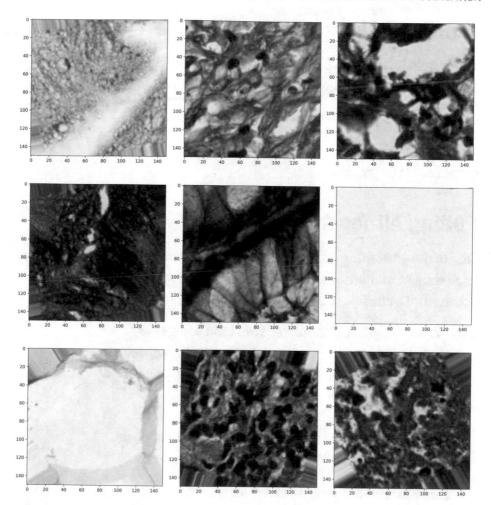

Figure 8-14. *The effect of rotating images in a random direction up to 40 degrees. The parts of the images left empty by the rotation have been filled with the nearest mode.*

Zooming in Images

You should now understand how these image transformations work. Zooming is as easy as the previous transformation:

```
datagen = ImageDataGenerator(zoom_range=0.2)

# fit parameters from data
datagen.fit(x_train)
```

Putting All Together

One of the great things about Keras is that you don't need to perform each transformation, one at a time. You can do everything in one shot. For example, consider this code:

```
datagen = ImageDataGenerator(rotation_range=40,
                             width_shift_range=0.2,
                             height_shift_range=0.2,
                             shear_range=0.2,
                             zoom_range=0.2,
                             horizontal_flip=True,
                             fill_mode="nearest")
```

This will enhance your dataset greatly, with several transformations done at the same time:

- Rotation

- Shift

- Shear

- Zoom

- Flip

Let's put everything together and see how effective this technique is.

VGG16 with Data Augmentation

Now it's time to train our vgg16 network with transfer learning and image augmentation. The only modification to the code we looked at before is in how we feed the data to train the model.

Now we will need to use this code:

```
history=model_vgg16_v4.fit_generator(datagen.flow(x_train,
y_train, batch_size=BATCH_SIZE),
                                    validation_data=(x_test,
                                    y_test),
                                    epochs=EPOCHS,
                                    callbacks=[checkpointer])
```

Instead of the classical fit() call, we need to use fit_generator(). A small digression is necessary to explain the main differences between the two functions. Keras includes not two, but three functions that can be used to train a model:

- fit()

- fit_generator()

- train_on_batch()

The fit( ) Function

Up to now, we used the fit() function when training our Keras models. The main implicit assumption when using this method is that the dataset that you feed to the model will fit completely in memory. We don't need to move batches to and from memory. That is a pretty big assumption, especially if you are working on big datasets and your laptop or desktop doesn't have a lot of memory available. Additionally, the assumption is that there is no need to do real-time data augmentation (as we want to do here).

> **Note**   The fit() function is good for small datasets that can fit in your system memory and do not require real-time data augmentation.

The fit_generator() Function

When the data does not fit in memory anymore, we need a smarter function that can help us deal with it. Note that the ImageDataGenerator we created before will generate, in a random fashion, batches that need to be fed to the model. The fit_generator() function assumes that there is a function that generates the data for it. When using fit_generator(), Keras follows this process:

1. Keras calls the function that generates the batches. In our code, that's datagen.flow().

2. This generator function returns a batch whose size is specified by the batch_size=BATCH_SIZE parameter.

3. The fit.generator() function then performs backpropagation and updates the weights.

4. This is repeated until we reach the number of epochs wanted.

> **Note**   The fit_generator() function is meant to be used for bigger datasets that do not fit in memory and when you need to do data augmentation.

Note that there is an important parameter that we have not used in our code: steps_per_epoch. The datagen.flow() function will generate a batch of images each time, but Keras needs to know how many such batches we want for each epoch, since the datagen.flow() can continue to generate as many batches as we want (remember that they are generated in a random fashion). We need to decide how many batches we want before declaring each epoch finished. You can decide with the steps_per_epoch parameter, but if you don't specify it, Keras will use len(generator)[5] as the number of steps.

The train_on_batch() Function

If you need to fine-tune your training, the train_on_batch() function is the one to use.

Note   The train_on_batch() function accepts a single batch of data, performs backpropagation, and then updates the model parameters.

The batch of data can be arbitrarily sized and can be theoretically in any format you need. You need this function when you need, for example, to perform custom data augmentation that cannot be done by the standard Keras functions.

Note   As they say—if you don't know whether you need the train_on_batch() function, you probably don't.

You can find more information from the official documentation at https://keras.io/models/sequential/.

---

[5]https://keras.io/models/sequential/

Training the Network

We can finally train our network and see how it performs. Training it for 50 epochs and with a batch size of 128 gives the following accuracies:

- Accuracy on the training dataset: 93.3%

- Accuracy on the validation dataset: 91%

That is a great result. Practically no overfitting and great accuracy. This network took roughly 15 minutes on Google Colab, which is quite fast. Figure 8-15 shows the accuracies and loss versus the number of epochs.

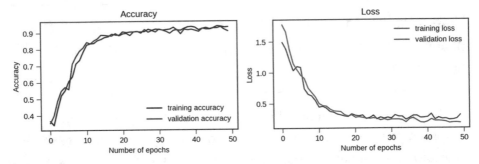

Figure 8-15. *Accuracy and loss function versus the number of epochs for the VGG16 network with transfer learning and data augmentation*

To summarize, we started with a simple CNN that was not too bad, but we immediately realized that going deeper (more layers) and increasing the complexity (more kernels) led to overfitting quite dramatically. Adding dropout was not really helping, so the only solution was to use data augmentation.

Note that we did not show the first networks described in this chapter with data augmentation for space reasons, but you should do that. If you try, you will realize that you fight overfitting quite efficiently, but the accuracy goes down. Using a pre-trained network gives us a very good starting point and allows us to go into the 90% accuracy regime in a few epochs.

And Now Have Fun...

In this book, you have learned powerful techniques that will allow you to read research papers, understand them, and start implementing more advanced networks that go beyond the easy CNNs that you find in blogs and websites. I hope you enjoyed the book and that it will help you in your journey toward deep learning mastery. Deep learning is really fun and an incredibly creative research field. I hope you now have a glimpse of the possibilities of the algorithms and the creativity involved. I love feedback and would love to hear from you. Don't hesitate to get in touch and tell me how (and especially if) this book has helped you learn those algorithms.

—Umberto Michelucci, Dübendorf, June 2019

Index

A

Adam optimizer, 33, 162
Anaconda
    benefits/drawbacks, 17–18
    download, 9
    install, 11–14
    screen, 10

B

BBox-Label-Tool, 240
Building blocks, CNN
    convolutional
        layer, 105–107
    pooling layer, 108
    stacking layers, 108, 109

C

call() function, 186
Chessboard image
    blurring kernel I_B, 95, 96
    creation, 91
    horizontal edges, 93
    kernel, I_H, 92, 93
    kernel, I_L, 94, 95
    kernel I_V, 94, 97
    transition, values, 98

Classification loss, 229
Confidence loss, 229
Content loss function, 179
Convolution
    definition, 85
    example, chessboard (*see*
        Chessboard image)
    kernel I_H, 86, 87
    kernels, 82
    matrix, 82, 83
    matrix 3×3, 88, 90
    multiple channels, 125–128
    Python, 90
    size, 85
    stride, 85, 87
    tensors, 81, 82
    visual explanation, 86
    works, 86
Convolutional neural
        network (CNN)
    building blocks (*see* Building
        blocks, CNN)
    visualization (*see* Visualization
        of CNN)
    weights
        convolutional layer, 109
        dense layer, 110
        pooling layer, 110

V, W, X

Y, Z

Printed in the United States
By Bookmasters